Cologne in the Twelfth Century

Cologne in the Twelfth Century

Paul Strait

A Florida State University Book

University Presses of Florida, Gainesville, 1974

Library of Congress Cataloging in Publication Data

Strait, Paul, 1940–
    Cologne in the twelfth century.

    "A Florida State University book."
    Bibliography: p.
    1. Cologne–History. I. Title.
    DD901.C76S85   309.1'43'55   74-1292
    ISBN 0-8130-0448-9

PRINTED IN THE UNITED STATES OF AMERICA

Contents

Abbreviations

AESC: Annales: Economies, Sociétés, Civilisations.

AHES: Annales d'Histoire Economique et Sociale.

AHR: American Historical Review.

Annalen: Annalen des historischen Vereins für den Niederrhein.

H: Hoeniger, Robert, ed. *Kölner Schreinskarten des zwölften Jahrhunderts.* 2 vols. Bonn: Weber, 1884—94.

Lacomblet: Lacomblet, Theodor, ed. *Urkundenbuch für die Geschichte des Niederrheins.* 4 vols. Düsseldorf: Elberfeld, 1840—58.

Mevissenfestschrift: Beiträge zur Geschichte vornehmlich Kölns und der Rheinlande zum achtzigsten Geburtstag Gustav von Mevissens. Köln: DuMont-Schauberg, 1895.

MGH. DD: Monumenta Germaniae Historica. Diplomata.

MGH. LL: Monumenta Germaniae Historica. Leges.

MGH. SS: Monumenta Germaniae Historica. Scriptores.

Mitteilungen: Mitteilungen aus dem Stadtarchiv von Köln.

RBPH: Revue Belge de Philologie et d'Histoire.

Quellen: Ennen, Leonhard, and Gottfried Eckertz, eds. *Quellen zur Geschichte der Stadt Köln.* 6 vols. Köln: DuMont- Schauberg, 1863—79.

VSWG: Vierteljahrschrift für Sozial- und Wirtschaftsgeschichte.

Von Loesch: Von Loesch, Heinrich, ed. *Die Kölner Zunfturkunden nebst anderen Kölner Gewerbeurkunden bis zum Jahre 1500.* 2 vols. Bonn: Hanstein, 1907.

ZRG: Zeitschrift der Savigny-Stiftung für Rechtsgeschichte. Germanistische Abteilung.

Chapter 1

An Introductory Note on the Sources

The twelfth is the first century for which there is extensive documentation from the urban community at Cologne. Before the second quarter of the century, and in earlier centuries, occasional documents issued by the archbishop or the king, or narrative sources betraying some knowledge of Cologne, must suffice; but after 1135 a series of urban records, drawn up by the townspeople themselves, release the urban community at Cologne from relative obscurity. These records are presently located in the city archives of Cologne.

The form and organization of the documents reveal much, even apart from their contents. Beginning around 1135, the officials in certain parishes began to keep records of various transactions on pieces of parchment. These are known today as *Schreinskarten* because the records were single sheets (*Karten* as opposed to the later *Bücher*) and because they were kept, apparently, in a box or chest (*scrinium* or *Schrein*) in the parish church. Early entries on these *Schreinskarten* are, on the whole, more explicit and more detailed than later entries. As more and more transactions were recorded in the course of the twelfth century, the entries tended to become regularized. They assumed more of the details of the transaction and were explicit only in regard to the names of the parties involved, the locations at issue, any sums involved, and witnesses, if any, in the appropriate places of more or less standard forms.

As the entries became more numerous, the *Schreinskarten* also became specialized. At first, certain sections of a given *Schreinskarte* received a designation of a particular street or district in a parish. By the last decade of the twelfth century, separate *Schreinskarten* were kept for these districts. For example, there are eight separate *Schreinskarten* for divisions of Martin parish covering the period from ca. 1190 to ca. 1220. Three additional *Schreinskarten* in Martin parish are specialized not by areas but by subject matter. Thus sheet 14, although not titled, contains securities on loans and other short-term transactions from the last decade of the twelfth century, and is the forerunner of sheets 23 and 24, entitled *vadimonia*, from the first half of the thirteenth century. Specialization in the *Schreinskarten* of other parishes tends to come a little later but has occurred in most of the important ones by 1240 or 1250. In virtually every parish by the middle of the thirteenth century the *Schreinskarten* were put together as books (*Schreinsbücher*).

Historians of Cologne and the Rhineland owe a great debt to the *Gesellschaft für rheinische Geschichtskunde*, which has published many printed sources. Among their projects is an almost complete series of the twelfth-century *Schreinskarten*, edited by Robert Hoeniger (*Kölner Schreinskarten des zwölften Jahrhunderts*, 2 vols. Bonn, 1884–94). To my knowledge, the only twelfth-century *Schreinskarten* missing in his edition are those more specialized ones from the 1190's. In 1937 Hans Planitz and Thea Buyken edited selections from the *Schreinsbücher* of the thirteenth and fourteenth centuries in the same series of publications (*Die Kölner Schreinsbücher des 13. und 14. Jahrhunderts*, Weimar, 1937). This volume is valuable in appreciating the scope and character of later records, but it is not a complete series of the *Schreinsbücher*. In addition to these printed sources, the manuscript collections of the later *Schreinskarten* and the earlier *Schreinsbücher* held in the Cologne City Archives have been examined; however, they have not substantially modified the conclusions suggested by the printed sources.

In addition to these urban records, other standard sources for the period have been used. Narrative sources have proved valuable for some major events, but the urban characters who are our chief concern seldom seemed important to a monastic chronicler. More significant are other nonnarrative sources: the records of the archbishopric, of the other ecclesiastical institutions in and around Cologne, and of the monarchy. Two printed source collections are particularly important here: Theodor Lacomblet, ed., *Urkundenbuch für die Geschichte des Niederrheins*, 4 vols. (Düsseldorf, 1840–58) and Leonhard Ennen and Gottfried Eckertz, eds., *Quellen zur Geschichte der Stadt Köln*, 6 vols. (Köln, 1863–79).

On the basis of these records, the present study attempts to elucidate the evolution of urban institutions and the men who made them work in twelfth-century Cologne.

Chapter 2

Elements of Urban Life in Pre-Urban Cologne

The Romans founded *Colonia Claudia Ara Agrippinensis* on the left bank of the Rhine about 50 or 55 A.D. Originally a veterans' settlement, Cologne flourished as a result of its position in the political structure of the empire and the economic needs of a new military and civilian population. The *Notitia Galliarum*, from the end of the fourth century, mentions Cologne as the capital of Lower Germany. Despite its political importance, Cologne seems never to have attained the military significance of its long-time rival Mainz, which was the seat of a military command as well as the political capital of Upper Germany. The *Notitia dignitatum orientalis et occidentalis*, a list roughly contemporary with the *Notitia Galliarum*, mentions no military command for Cologne. The chief military strongpoint in Lower Germany was farther down the Rhine near Xanten.[1] Nevertheless, Cologne was a fortified city. The old Roman wall, parts of which are still today the object of excavation in Cologne, lasted well into the Middle Ages. The area of the Roman city was much smaller than that of the medieval city, and the population was presumably smaller as well.

The Frankish period was a period of decline for the city of Cologne as it was for other northern towns. The Frankish invaders, who conquered Cologne for the first time shortly before 356 and then finally in 406, regarded the city chiefly as an object of booty.[2] Whatever the

---

1. Karl Hegel, *Die Entstehung des deutschen Städtewesens* (Leipzig, 1898), pp.1–4; Richard Koebner, *Die Anfänge des Gemeinwesens der Stadt Köln* (Bonn, 1922), p.51.

2. Hegel, pp.4–7; Koebner, p.54. Joseph Klersch, *Volkstum und Volksleben in Köln* (Köln, 1965), I, p.10, dates the final conquest of Cologne by the Franks from about 485. The disinclination of the Franks

3

precise tempo of economic change from the fifth to the tenth century,[3] the direction of change is clear: the towns lost economic importance and population. The Romans had diverted the Rhine into a channel to afford Cologne good harbor facilities. The necessities of border defense in the fourth century had led them to establish a fortress at Deutz on the right bank of the Rhine opposite Cologne and a bridge connecting the two. These installations served no purpose in the Frankish period. The channel was allowed to silt up, turning the once flourishing harbor area into a marsh. The bridge fell, and Cologne and Deutz retained their separate identities. There may have been an attempt to encourage commercial expansion under the Carolingians, but it came to nothing.

---

to urban life is a constant theme in the German literature on the subject. It has been emphasized again by the best recent work on the precommunal phase of town development in Germany: Edith Ennen, *Frühgeschichte der europäischen Stadt* (Bonn, 1953), pp.85ff. and passim. The same author in an article "The Different Types of Formation of European Towns," in *Early Medieval Society*, translated and edited by Sylvia Thrupp (New York, 1967), p.175, points out that the Franks on the middle Rhine and the Moselle were less destructive to urban life than the Alemans on the upper Rhine and the Danube.

3. The older view, often attacked and largely discredited, is that of Pirenne. The famous "Pirenne thesis" has engendered so many words of criticism and defense that it would be impossible to review them all here, but the modification of Pirenne's periodization by Robert Latouche, *The Birth of the Western Economy*, translated by E. M. Wilkinson (London, 1961), should be mentioned. Latouche does not regard the Carolingian period as one of total decline. The Carolingians recognized the disastrous economic system they had inherited and set about to rectify it through currency reforms, market foundations, and economic regulation. The invasions of the later Carolingian period put an end to this hopeful beginning, in Latouche's view, and postponed urban development until the eleventh century.

Two of the points made by Latouche are of particular importance for Germany. First, the seat of Carolingian power in the Rhenish area and the expansion eastward encouraged economic development in Germany. "Trade increased by leaps and bounds in ninth-century Germany, which was becoming more civilized and was growing to be an integral part of the Frankish Empire" (Latouche, p.171). Second, the eastern part of the old empire recovered much more rapidly after the invasions than the western part. Ottonian economic policy was neo-Carolingian. The security of a relatively stable political order was important, but Latouche emphasizes also the role of the kings and emperors in market foundation and attempts at currency control.

No one today would stress the basic continuity between Roman and medieval towns, but the very dominance of this interpretation based on discontinuity has led many historians to look for those elements of continuity that do link the medieval town to the Roman town.[4]

Urban life in some form, however attenuated, never completely disappeared at Cologne. Archaeological discoveries since World War II have shown "that the city did not become a desolate field of rubble on which the only activity was farmers grazing their cattle."[5] Merchants remained, though these were principally Frisians or Jews and not Franks.[6] Some production by artisans was also maintained within the city, but the Frankish invasions had led to a considerable dislocation of most industrial production. The glassworks, located in Cologne in Roman times, were moved to the countryside after the invasions, and production was frequently by dependents of ecclesiastical foundations. The pottery industry also became more a rural than an urban undertaking.[7] Some Rhenish glassware has been found in Scandinavia, which suggests that these country artisans did not produce exclusively for a local market;[8] and either they or artisans still resident in Cologne must account for the objects found in recent excavations. A consider-

---

4. Klersch, p.11; Latouche, p.251, points out that discontinuity in urban development is generally accepted by recent German scholars, among them Edith Ennen. Ennen does confirm the views of Pirenne and Vercauteren that the Carolingian age marks the low point of urban life in Europe and the high point of lordship organization (*Frühgeschichte*, p.91). But she also emphasizes elements of continuity, especially with regard to religious life and ecclesiastical organization. Franz Steinbach, "Zur Sozialgeschichte von Köln im Mittelalter," *Spiegel der Geschichte: Festgabe für Max Braubach zum 10. April 1964* (Münster, 1964), emphasizes the elements of continuity even more stongly.

5. Steinbach, "Zur Sozialgeschichte," p.175; Koebner, p.63.

6. Steinbach, "Zur Sozialgeschichte," p.174; Latouche, pp.135, 260. The *platea Frisonum*, significantly, was not on the side of Cologne near the river, but outside the Roman walls on the west: cf. Klersch, p.33. This indicates the discontinuity between the Carolingian period and the later period. The mercantile *portus* in Cologne in the High Middle Ages was between the old Roman walls and the river in the east. The Jews lived principally in what was to become Lawrence parish next to the palace of the archbishop.

7. Ennen, *Frühgeschichte*, pp.89–90. She describes the Franks as the leading glassmakers of the Early Middle Ages.

8. Latouche, p.135.

able number of nonclerical Christians continued to live in Cologne after the invasions, and it is probable that they were artisans, small shopkeepers, and the like.[9] Still, emphasis on continued mercantile or industrial activity in Cologne is only a qualification of the generally valid interpretation that the economic life of the city declined precipitously.

Much more important as an element of continuity was the religious life of the city. Christians were more numerous than is sometimes supposed in the Roman cities of the Rhineland, and they did not disappear during or after the invasions of the heathen Franks.[10] Cologne remained what it had been before in the religious sphere, a "cultic" center. Before the Romans came, there had been pagan holy places and shrines in Cologne. The Roman name of Cologne itself indicates the significance of the altar dedicated to the worship of Roma and Augustus. This cultic importance remained in the Christian era, but now martyrs or saints were honored rather than pagan deities. The *locus sacer* tended to persist from early pagan times into the Christian Middle Ages. Archaeological studies have shown a general pattern of development in which a pagan *locus sacer* became the grave site of a martyr in the Christian era. On this spot a memorial shrine arose, then later a martyr's church, and finally, in the High Middle Ages, a chapter devoted to the memory of the martyr. St. Ursula, St. Gereon, and St. Severin in Cologne follow this pattern. These elements of religious continuity are not the outworn remnants of an old order but the growing and dynamic elements of a new order. To emphasize the religious rather than the industrial-commercial continuity is not to grasp at straws but to discuss something of vitality.[11] The religious centers provided a point of attraction to Cologne even when it had lost most of its earlier economic and political importance. The attraction of religious observances, along with relatively warmer and less muddy surroundings, even led many

---

9. Steinbach, "Zur Sozialgeschichte," p.174. He emphasizes the distinction between Christian artisans and shopkeepers and non-Christian and foreign merchants.

10. Ennen, *Frühgeschichte*, p.103; Ennen, "The Different Types of Formation," p.176; Steinbach, "Zur Sozialgeschichte," p.174.

11. Ennen, *Frühgeschichte*, p.104. See the literature cited there. These collegial churches did not become the actual nuclei of town development, as seems to have happened at Bonn, for example. Cf. Ennen, "The Different Types of Formation," p.176.

Carolingian rulers to spend their winters in a town rather than on a country estate.[12]

Urban life, then, never totally disappeared at Cologne. Christian artisans and shopkeepers, Jewish and Frisian merchants, clerics attached to the cathedral or to a church in the memory of a saint, perhaps even dependents of the Frankish count, remained resident in Cologne in the period between the Frankish invasions and the Ottonian revival, from the fifth to the tenth century. Cologne did not assume the agricultural appearance sometimes attributed to Mainz, and the area within the old Roman fortifications was not divided up into peasant village communities as occurred at Trier.[13] Nevertheless, the elements of continuity present in the Frankish period are insufficient to explain the rise of the medieval town of Cologne. The increased productivity of agriculture and the expansion of commerce in the eleventh and twelfth centuries created new conditions for urban development. Two aspects of this complex process are of particular importance here: the political leadership of the archbishop and the economic leadership of a new group of merchants.

As Roman institutions disappeared in the *civitates*, the power and authority of the resident bishop increased. He performed the minimal governmental functions of the age and made himself an indispensable figure in what life was left in the old *civitates*. In Cologne, political authority was shared with the local Frankish count or *Gaugraf*. The *comes Coloniae* is mentioned frequently in the ninth century from the reign of Louis the Pious on; one count, a certain Werner, is indicated by name in 849.[14] He was undoubtedly an itinerant official whose activities led him throughout the *Kölngau* even though he may have resided in Cologne. In any case, Cologne was no longer the administrative center it had been under the Romans, and the court belonged more properly to the countryside than to the town. The archbishop remained

---

12. Latouche, p.174.

13. Koebner, p.63, contrasts an agricultural Mainz to an urban Cologne in Carolingian times; but Latouche, pp.171, 253, indicates evidence of trade in Mainz at least by the ninth century; and even Koebner, p.205, admits the importance of Mainz as a market under the Carolingians. (Cf. also Etienne Saabe, "Quelques types de marchands des IXe et Xe siècles," *RBPH* 13 (1934), pp.176–87.) For Trier, cf. Ennen, *Frühgeschichte*, p.91 and the literature cited there.

14. *Werinarius comes Coloniae* is mentioned in the "Annales Colonienses Brevissimi," *MGH. SS.* I, p.97. Some have wanted to see him as a ninth-century *Burggraf*, but it is more likely that he was a latter-day *Gaugraf*. Cf. Steinbach, "Zur Sozialgeschichte," p.172.

the chief political leader in Cologne, and it was probably he who supervised the rebuilding of the fortifications of Cologne in 883 after the Norman invasions of 881.[15]

The de facto leadership of the bishop, which had developed naturally, was further strengthened in the ninth and tenth centuries through royal grants of immunities and regalian rights. The reliance of Carolingian and Ottonian rulers on the Church is well-known. The major portion of the *diplomata* of the Ottonian emperors concerns new grants and the confirmation of old grants to bishops and abbots. These vary widely from the very extensive privileges given by Otto I and his successors to the Church of St. Maurice in Magdeburg to more limited and partial grants, such as the right to collect a toll in one place or the right to have a mint in another.

Although documentary evidence is lacking for Cologne, it is generally assumed that similar grants were made to St. Peter's at Cologne during the reign of Archbishop Bruno (953–965), if not before. Bruno was the brother of Otto I and had been Otto's confidant before his election as archbishop; he is mentioned frequently in Otto's charters as an intercessor in behalf of various individuals and groups and as a general counselor. After his election, he retained his central position in the activities of the new state. He became not only archbishop of Cologne, but also duke of Lorraine; and, when Otto had to turn to troubles on the eastern frontier, Bruno was made *tutor* and *provisor* of the West, according to his contemporary biographer.[16] Since Otto was generous to

---

15. Ennen, *Frühgeschichte*, p.101. On the refortification of Cologne in 883, cf. "Annales Fuldenses," *MGH. SS.* I, p.398. In 881 Cologne had been burned by the Normans, and the clergy had fled with their treasure and relics to Mainz (ibid., p.394). In 883, Cologne is described as refortified: Agripina Colonia absque aecclesiis et monasteriis reaedificata, et muri eius cum portis et vectibus et seris instaurati.

This reference from 883 in Cologne deserves to be included in the series of examples given by Latouche, pp.174–5, that show Carolingian bishops were concerned with the development of the town and its buildings.

16. A number of chroniclers refer to Bruno's ducal powers. The clearest explanation is given in Ruotger, "Vita Brunonis," *MGH. SS.* IV, p.261. Otto left Bruno in charge of the West as a sort of "archduke" while he attended to problems in the East: ... fratrem suum Brunonem occidenti tutorem et provisorem, et ut ita dicam archiducem, in tam periculoso tempore misit. ... Ruotger also says that Bruno undertook royal affairs on imperial authority among the Lotharingians (ibid., p.263).

The "Continuator Reginonis," *MGH. SS.* I, p.622, describes Bruno as the duke of (Upper and Lower) Lotharingia: ... Brun, frater regis ...

other churches, it seems likely that the basis of the local territorial lordship enjoyed by the archbishop of Cologne in the eleventh and twelfth centuries was laid at the time of Archbishop Bruno.

Although a charter does not exist, certain aspects of the archbishop's authority can be established. He had a mint in Cologne, delegated to him by the royal authority. The coins minted there had Bruno's name on one side and the emperor's name on the other.[17] Some royal regulation of the mint still existed, but this disappeared as the mint passed into the hands of the archbishop and much later into those of the town. A market was also established in Cologne in the tenth century. It is first mentioned in a charter of Otto III in 994, but it is older. The imperial protection and rights granted to the merchants of Cologne served as a model for similar grants to other groups of merchants, such as those of Quedlinburg in 994.[18] With the market the

totius Lothariensis regni ducatum et regimen cum episcopatu suscepit.

If indeed Bruno had been the duke of Lotharingia, he lost his duchy in 959 (Koebner, pp.114–5). The description given by Ruotger of a sort of extraordinary command emphasizes the most important aspect of his title. Although the duchy was taken from Bruno, the later archbishops retained the ducal title and presumably maintained control of *Ripuaria*, the area immediately surrounding Cologne on the left bank of the Rhine.

17. Karl Theodor Eheberg, *Ueber das ältere deutsch Münzwesen und die Hausgenossenschaften besonders in volkswirtschaftlicher Beziehung* (Leipzig, 1879), pp.20–1. The practice of putting the archbishop's name on one side of the coin was discontinued under Bruno's immediate successors although they retained income rights in the mint. Under Archbishop Pilgrim, beginning in 1022, the procedure begun under Bruno was revived. Sometimes the emperor's name was even missing, an exception that became the rule by the end of Pilgrim's reign. On royal regulation see Charles-Edmond Perrin, "L'évolution d'une monnaie: le denier de Cologne," *AHES* 4 (1932), pp.194–7.

18. *MGH. DD.* II (Otto III), p.566: . . . omnique in mercatorio iure, quod antecessorum nostrorum industria Coloniae, Magontiae et Magadaburch videbatur esse concessum.

Latouche, pp.246–51, places renewed emphasis on market foundation as an important step in town formation although, as he is well aware, the theory that hoped to establish the market as the single most important factor is largely discredited. His remarks are certainly sensible, at least for Germany. Hans Planitz, "Kaufmannsgilde und städtische Eidgenossenschaft in niederfränkischen Städten im 11. und 12. Jahrhundert," *ZRG* 60 (1940), pp.103–4, distinguishes carefully in interpreting the reference to Cologne above between *ius fori* and *ius mercatorum*. It is merchant law, not market law, that is indicated here.

archbishop received certain tolls and levies. In addition to market tolls, he levied tolls at various places along the Rhine, including the important fortress of Andernach, which was granted to Rainald of Dassel in 1167.[19]

Political and judicial authority also passed to the archbishop. As noted, grants of immunity to cathedrals and monasteries were quite common in the tenth century. Such a grant prevented any regular royal official from interfering for any public reason in the lands of the ecclesiastical foundation involved and gave the recipient political control over the inhabitants in the affected lands.[20] The Frankish count, still mentioned as the *comes Coloniae* in the ninth century, disappears in the tenth century. The archbishop had managed to exclude him from the town and the area surrounding it, the so-called *Burgbann* or *districtio urbis* of Cologne. The former count of the *Kölngau* now became the count of the *Gillgau*. The ban of the archbishop (the *Burgbann*) extended beyond the city walls, and he had effective control in this area.[21] The ban involved the rights of high justice, and, since the

---

19. Lacomblet I 426.

20. Otto I granted a large number of such privileges. There is considerable variety in the extent of the rights granted, at least in the formulas employed in the charters. In 937 the archbishop of Hamburg was given an immunity over "litis . . . et colonis" (*MGH. DD*. I, no.11); in the same year the bishop of Halberstadt had his immunity confirmed over "litos aut colonos seu quoslibet viros ad ipsam sedem variis modis inquisitos vel adhuc adquirendos . . . " (ibid., no.7); in 965 the archbishop of Hamburg was given immunity control over the merchants resident in the new market of Bremen (ibid., no.307); and in 958 half the city of Chur was given to the bishop "cum tali districtione et iure sicuti hactenus ad nostram pertinebat potestatem et sicuti homines ipsius totius provinciae censuales ac liberi debitores sunt. . . . " (ibid., no.191).

21. Franz Steinbach, *Der Ursprung der Kölner Stadtgemeinde* (Bonn, 1955), pp.3—4. Steinbach has also shown, on the basis of thirteenth-century evidence, that the archbishop continued to limit the jurisdiction of the *Gaugraf* and consequently acquired direct jurisdiction over an area beyond the *Burgbann*, an area called the *Bannmeile*. In 1237 the archbishop had the emperor and the princes of the empire confirm his right to hold court within the *Bannmeile*. At issue at that time was whether Cologne burghers could be called out to an archiepiscopal court in the village of Bell, a place outside the *Burgbann* but within the *Bannmeile*. The burghers won this conflict in 1239 when Archbishop Conrad gave up the right to summon burghers to courts outside the town. But the dispute clearly shows that the *Burgbann* and the *Bannmeile* were not the same

archbishop could not shed blood, he had to appoint a layman to head the court. In most bishoprics this was the advocate of the cathedral (the *Domvogt*), but in Cologne the power of exercising the ban was vested in a *Burggraf*.[22] Although the *Burggraf* is mentioned for the first time in 1032, it is probable that the office was established in the tenth century when the *Gaugraf* was excluded from Cologne. The *Burggraf*, a noble from the countryside, was named by the archbishop, but he was granted the ban itself by the king.[23] Criminal justice was exercised by the *Burggraf's* court throughout the *Burgbann*; however, civil justice had to be shared with the courts of the *Stadtvogt* and the abbot of St. Martin within the city and, especially, with the old ecclesiastical foundations, such as St. Pantaleon and St. Gereon, which lay outside the walls of the city but within the *Burgbann*.[24]

The other officials of the archbishop's court in Cologne cannot be documented until the twelfth century although they may well be older. The *Stadtvogt* or *advocatus urbis* occupied a position analogous to that of the *Schultheiss* in other Rhenish episcopal cities and is not to be confused with the *Domvogt*, who was excluded from urban affairs in Cologne.[25] He did not receive a ban for high justice, and his activity

---

thing. Steinbach explains this by holding that after Bruno had separated the *Burgbann* from the *Kölngau* the archbishops continued to limit the powers of the *Gaugraf*, excluding him from an area south and southwest of Cologne and making him feudally dependent for the area north of Cologne. This new area placed under the archbishop's direct control was, presumably, the *Bannmeile* – although by the thirteenth century this is obscured somewhat by the existence of special jurisdictions that had developed since the tenth century. Most earlier writers had assumed that the *Burgbann* and the *Bannmeile* were identical.

22. Friedrich Lau, *Entwicklung der kommunalen Verfassung und Verwaltung der Stadt Köln bis zum Jahre 1396* (Bonn, 1898), p.5. An *advocatus* of the bishop is mentioned frequently in the immunity charters. In most Rhenish cities, at least, this *advocatus* was the *Domvogt*. Cf. Elisabeth Rütimeyer, *Stadtherr und Stadtbürgerschaft in den rheinischen Bischofsstädten* (Stuttgart, 1928), pp.148,178.

23. Lacomblet I 167 (1032); Lau, *Entwicklung*, p.8 The position of the *Burggraf* as a vassal of the bishop, who received his judicial power as a fief from the bishop, but also was conferred a royal ban by the king, is the same as that of the *Domvögte* in the other cities. Cf. Rütimeyer, p.148.

24. Lau, *Entwicklung*, p.5; Steinbach, *Ursprung der Kölner Stadtgemeinde* p.6.

25. Rütimeyer, p.179.

was primarily confined to lesser cases. In addition to the *Burggraf* and the *Stadtvogt*, who presided over the court, there were *scabini*, who assisted in the court sessions. The *scabini* are mentioned for the first time in 1103,[26] but it is generally assumed that they were established much earlier. The first *scabini* we can identify in the twelfth century come, naturally enough, from the town of Cologne, the area under the jurisdiction of the court.

By the beginning of the twelfth century the archbishop's lordship in the area of Cologne was of long standing and secure. It was exercised by the officials of the court, the *Burggraf*, the *Stadtvogt*, and the *scabini*. But over whom did they exercise their authority? Was Cologne organized like an agricultural *villa* with a few concessions made to the merchants resident within its walls? Had personal freedom and free land tenures disappeared for all practical purposes in Cologne in the tenth and eleventh centuries? Or was there a continuity of free men in Cologne?

There is little doubt that the archbishop came to regard Cologne as "his" city. His leadership was extended over the city as it was over many of the neighboring areas. But the very continuity of urban life in Cologne and the continued existence of free men made it difficult to regard Cologne as just another *villa*. The archbishop could distinguish quite clearly between the *familia* of the cathedral and the free men resident in the town. The court of the *Burggraf*, with *scabini* chosen from among the more honorable inhabitants of the town was itself a kind of public court exercising its authority over free men. The *Stadtvogt*, despite his ministerial status and functions, exercised a similar jurisdiction on the basis of a lower court. There is no doubt that the development of the merchant community was a major factor in populating Cologne with free men, but there was a tradition on which to build.

There was a greater number of dependent persons in Cologne before the thirteenth century than thereafter. The suburbs of the old Roman *civitas* were *villae* subject to the lordship of ecclesiastical foundations such as St. Pantaleon, St. Gereon, and St. Severin. Within the walls, the abbot of St. Martin and the prioress of St. Maria ad Gradus each had his or her own *familia* and even collected an entry fee into some properties in the mercantile suburb. Twelfth-century residents of Cologne are frequently described as belonging to the *familia* of one of these ecclesiastical foundations or as being *ministeriales* or *homines* of them. The specific problem will be considered later, but in most cases such a

---

26. *Quellen* I 601.

dependent status was not incompatible with a bourgeois status in the twelfth century.

The archbishop also had his *familia*. The chamberlain was the official responsible for the archbishop's income from the mint and tolls and from the *familia* itself. In Cologne he was a layman rather than a member of the cathedral chapter.[27] In a number of court cases in the twelfth century, the chamberlain tried to claim that various inhabitants of the town and their progeny pertained to the episcopal *curia*. Such a charge, for instance, was brought against Udelgard, the wife of Waldever the viscount, and all her progeny in the 1160's. Invariably the chamberlain lost these cases by decision of the *scabini*.[28] Although it is impossible even to guess at percentages, it is probably safe to assume that the cases in the twelfth century concerning dependents are the last remnants of a system that had wider currency in the city in the tenth and eleventh centuries. To admit this is not to exclude the probability that a free community under the authority of the archbishop and of the *Burggraf* continued to exist at Cologne in this period; however, it was not this free community or the dependents of the archbishop that gave the chief impetus to urban development at Cologne. The development of the archbishop's lordship was the first step in establishing the medieval town of Cologne; the second was the development of a new group of merchants.

Cologne followed the classic *portus* development. In the ninth or tenth century, probably soon after the Norman invasion of 881, a new group of merchants and artisans settled in the area between the old Roman fortifications and the Rhine. Sometime in the tenth century this new area was included in the fortifications system and became a part of the *civitas Coloniensis* in the narrower sense. The market located in this area is the one mentioned in the charter of Otto III for Quedlinburg in 994. A discontinuity in physical location is matched by a discontinuity in the merchants themselves. In the previous period most merchants had been Frisians or Jews. The Frisians were located outside the walls in the

---

27. Friedrich Lau, *Die erzbischöflichen Beamten in der Stadt Köln während des zwölften Jahrhunderts* (Lübeck, 1891), p.46.

28. H. II, p.294: Notum sit quod camerarius Hermannus Udhelgardem uxorem Waldeveri comitis in curia super iure suo gravavit, dicens tam eam quam sobolem in curiam episcopalem pertinere. . . . This is an entry in the registry of the *scabini*. A similar charge was brought against Mathilda of Niederich in the period 1155–65, and she was adjudged free by the senator Antonius (H. II, p.293). A similar case was decided in communal court against the son of the duke of Limburg in the 1190's (H. II, p.301).

Platea Frisonum on the other side of the city; the Jewish community was within the walls near the archbishop's palace in what was to become St. Lawrence parish. The new merchants were Germans, not Frisians or Jews.[29]

The location of the mercantile *portus* is significant. It lay on the gently sloping land leading down to the Rhine outside the old Roman walls. Much of the land was low-lying and marshy, necessitating drainage to make it suitable for habitation. But it had one major advantage: it was on the river. The Rhine, of course, was a major artery in long-distance trade, and that trade gave the mercantile quarter of St. Martin the preeminence it enjoyed. Already in the tenth century the wine trade from the Rhine and Moselle regions was of importance, and early in the Middle Ages Cologne smiths were importing iron from Westphalia to manufacture weapons. Eventually copper and gold products also achieved some importance. In the eleventh century cloth from Cologne was distributed widely by Cologne merchants, and it was still a rival for Flemish cloth.[30] But Cologne remained principally a commercial, not an industrial center. The wine trade, especially, seems to have been the basis of her prosperity. The importance of Cologne in the twelfth-century trade of northwestern Europe is indicated by the privileges granted by English kings to "merchants from Cologne and other Germans" and by the wide circulation of the Cologne penny as a means of international exchange.[31]

As the urban community developed in the twelfth century and the old lordship organization declined, the *Burggraf* and the *Stadtvogt* gradually lost their rights in the town. What is known about the specific activities of the *Burggraf* and *Stadtvogt* comes principally from the late twelfth century or the thirteenth century when the offices were rapidly

---

29. Some Frisians and Jews became part of the new burgher community. One of the prominent twelfth-century *scabini* was Gottfried of Staveren. Names can frequently be misleading, but Staveren is in Frisia. More conclusive evidence exists for Jews, especially for those converted to Christianity. The clearest example comes from St. Lawrence parish, in which the Jewish community was located. In a list of parish officials from the period 1135–52, three out of twelve are designated "Judeus" (H. I, p.218). These are probably converts. This is clearly the case for Eckbert and his son Fordolf. Eckbert is described in another list of officials from St. Lawrence as Eckbert "qui Judeus fuit" (H. I, p.218).

30. Ennen, *Frühgeschichte*, p.147; Latouche, p.256; Koebner, p.203; Planitz, "Kaufmannsgilde und städtische Eidgenossenschaft," pp.9–10.

31. Perrin, p.195.

losing any authority they previously had, but most of these activities presumably go back at least to the eleventh century. The most important source for the duties and the rights of the two officials, especially the *Burggraf*, is a document that purports to come from the year 1169 but actually was forged sometime around 1230.[32] According to the text of the document, an old charter defining the rights of the *Burggraf*, scarcely legible from its great age, was discovered among the town records. Although this is a transparent attempt to lend age and authority to what in fact were innovations, most of the provisions concerning the *Burggraf* can be confirmed from other sources.

In the document the *Burggraf* is depicted most prominently in a judicial role. He is the archbishop's advocate in blood judgments, who presides over the three general courts by himself and who, along with the archbishop, holds the ban from the empire.[33] This agrees with the judicial position of the *Burggraf* described above; however, the document also gives him a court concerning hereditary properties in Cologne (*iudicium de hereditatibus infra Coloniam sitis*). This was probably a residual claim from an earlier period. The *Burggraf* did occasionally take action in property cases this late, but by 1230 the burghers controlled the transfer of property. The *Burggraf* also has authority over public lands including the right to tear down structures that had infringed upon public ways. Primarily, this concerned shops and stalls that extended into the streets, and the *Burggraf* was still exercising this power in the early thirteenth century.[34] In addition to his judicial and other public

---

32. *Quellen* I 76. Gerhard Seeliger, *Studien zur älteren Verfassungsgeschichte Köln: Zwei Urkunden des Kölner Erzbischofs von 1169* (Leipzig, 1909) and Konrad Beyerle, *Die Urkundenfälschungen des Kölner Burggrafen Heinrich III. von Arberg* (Heidelberg, 1913) attribute the forgery to the *Burggraf* himself.

33. These provisions also appear in a document of 1169 defining the rights of the *Stadtvogt* (*Quellen* I 77) which Seeliger also considers a forgery. It is difficult to be certain, however, since we have only a later copy of the document.

34. There are at least two examples of the *Burggraf's* activity in 1231. One case involves the guarantee that no way (*nulla via nec transitus*) shall be made through the houses or lands of a Cologne household. This is probably an example of the *Burggraf's* control of public ways. The other case involves property obtained by the convent of the Maccabees "per uoluntatem scabinorum et officialium de Niderich et per consensum burggrauii Colon." The court officials of Niederich are the dominant group here apparently, but at least the consent of the *Burggraf* is included. Both cases are printed in *Quellen* II 124.

functions, the *Burggraf* is given considerable control over the *scabini*. He is to install them and to be sure that they are good men who are not infirm or criminal or less than twenty-four years old. Each *scabinus* is to pay the *Burggraf* an entry fee of one mark and one measure of grain. He also has income specified from the mint, the Jews, and the citizens themselves as well as one-fourth of the judicial income, the rest going to the archbishop.

In addition to the provisions directly involving the *Burggraf*, the document contains two clauses affecting the burghers: the right to freedom from tolls at all tollstations of the archbishop and the right not to be summoned (*ius de non evocando*) to a court outside Cologne. This issue of the *ius de non evocando* was of great importance and still very much in dispute as the events of 1237 and 1239 mentioned above show. It has been suggested that the *Burggraf* had the document forged and included the provisions favoring the burghers to gain their support. His motive is supposed to have been the *iudicium de hereditatibus*. Possibly he was trying to acquire a share of the property jurisdiction in Cologne, which had become increasingly important in the twelfth century. If, as appears likely, the *iudicium de hereditatibus* is simply a later reference to an earlier jurisdiction of his, then it is probable that the burghers themselves had the document forged. For the rest, the *Burggraf* appears as the chief official of high justice in Cologne with various incomes derived from public duties or prerogatives and the control of public places in the town. With the growth of communal institutions much of this had been lost by the thirteenth century when the document was forged, but it represented his position in the eleventh century fairly accurately.[35]

By the early twelfth century the lordship principle represented in the court of the *Burggraf* began to give way to a communal principle. The

---

A clear example of the *Räumungsrecht* of the *Burggraf* is given in Lacomblet II 220 (1237): . . . ego Henricus Burgrauius Coloniensis de consilio et consensu scabinorum coloniensium vendidi ciuibus colon. scilicet ecclesiis tam clericis quam laicis qui domos habent sitas colonie in vico qui dicitur undir gedemin, officium siue ius meum quod habeo in demoliendo siue frangendo ea que colonie in domibus et edificiis sunt ante edificata, que vulgariter dicitur vorgezimbere. . . . The precise definition of the area given makes it appear that the *Burggraf* was still exercising his *Räumungsrecht* in other parts of the city at this time.

35. Lau, *Entwicklung*, pp.9—11, gives a summary of the rights and duties of the *Burggraf*.

merchants of Cologne and their distinctive institutions were undoubtedly responsible for much of this new development; but, as we shall see, the judicial community attached to the court of the *Burggraf*, and even the personal dependents of the archbishop, played a part in the origin of the new urban community at Cologne.

Chapter 3

Origins of the Urban Community at Cologne

For well over a century historians have developed theories to explain the origins of the European urban communities of the eleventh and twelfth centuries. Cologne and towns like it, which had a long if uneven history before the eleventh century and a complex institutional development after it, have often been given too little attention. It has been easier on the whole to develop a theory based on towns that had simpler histories and then apply it to towns like Cologne, emphasizing those elements in Cologne's rich history that fit the theory and minimizing those that do not.[1] Since Cologne was undeniably one of the leading commercial centers of the period in northwestern Europe and since it also enjoyed political influence early, it is reasonable to study the origins of the urban community at Cologne on its own terms. Reference must be made to past and present theories, but they must not bind our conclusions.

One important presupposition underlies the present study: bourgeois groups should not be considered in a vacuum; they should not be treated as aliens in a hostile society, as creative spirits who heralded, however much before its time, a new age. The group of historians associated generally with the theories of Henri Pirenne too often view the burghers as aliens or as harbingers of things to come. Recent historical scholarship has sought to correct this failure of perspective. Rural landlords could be as aggressive and as shrewd as any merchant; they could and did hold their own in an expanding economy. In Germany the *ministeriales* could and did participate in the life of the town politically and economically, not as the representatives of a principle alien to bourgeois communal life but as full partners of the

---

1. Cf. the comments of Koebner, p.4.

18

mercantile burghers from whom they are often indistinguishable.[2] The distinction drawn between townsmen and lords, and especially the one between burghers and *ministeriales*, on the basis of a supposed difference in attitudes and values is misleading. Urban society and rural society in a given region should not be completely separate as objects of study.

Because Cologne developed early into the leading commercial city in Germany, most of the first stages of urban development are difficult to ascertain. Some of the original merchants at Cologne may have been the itinerant outcasts Pirenne has described. Certainly the *portus* area of St. Martin was an *entrepôt* for long-distance trade. Probably the merchants at Cologne also derived from the other sources for the early medieval merchant class.[3] The documentary sources for Cologne itself come from a later period when the town community had already developed. By the end of the eleventh century, merchants resided in all parishes of Cologne, not only in St. Martin, and many did not belong to the merchant gild.[4] Nor were all burghers merchants. The term *burgensis* has been taken back not to the Germanic *Burg* but to the Latin use of the word *burgum* or *burgus*, referring to a mercantile suburb. Thus the increasing use of *burgensis* in the twelfth century is often seen as an indication of the predominant role the mercantile inhabitants of the *burgus* played in town development. But here, as in so many cases, Cologne is an exception. The mercantile suburb was already included in the urban fortification system in the tenth century. When the term was applied in the twelfth century, it could apply to any property holder within the town, especially to the *scabini* and other men of their rank.[5]

---

2. Ronald G. Witt, "The Landlord and the Economic Revival of the Middle Ages in Northern Europe, 1000–1250," *AHR* 76 (1971), pp.965–88; Knut Schulz, "Die Ministerialität als Problem der Stadtgeschichte," *Rheinische Vierteljahrsblätter* 32 (1968), pp.184–219; Knut Schulz, *Ministerialität und Bürgertum in Trier: Untersuchungen zur rechtlichen und sozialen Gliederung der Trierer Bürgerschaft* (Bonn, 1969).

3. Saabe, pp.176–87, has identified a variety of mercantile types for the Early Middle Ages.

4. This is the reason Planitz, "Kaufmannsgilde und städtische Eidgenossenschaft," p.29, thinks that the *Richerzeche* supplanted the merchant gild in Cologne. See below, Chapter 4.

5. Ennen, *Frühgeschichte* pp. 124–9, discusses the use of the term *burgensis*; she admits that Cologne constitutes an exception. In following discussions the term *burgher* will denote a person who holds property in

The development in Cologne was so early that distinctions of this sort cannot be tested there.

One distinction that is useful in understanding the development of Cologne is that there are two general types of town development in northern Europe in the Middle Ages: the new towns, for which the Pirenne thesis may be adequate, and the towns formed around old *civitates* or Carolingian abbeys, for which it is not adequate.[6] The main difference in the second type of development is that the "pre-urban nucleus" was not nearly so passive. By the tenth century in Cologne, the *civitas* had already absorbed the *portus*. In Cologne, at least, the dualism between the "pre-urban nucleus" and the mercantile suburb gave way rather early to the fortified town.

Scholarly opinions differ widely on the origins of the urban community at Cologne. The two historians who have studied Cologne most recently have discerned the origins of the commune in either the

---

the city and therefore comes under urban jurisdiction. This seems to be the definition of the term most closely approximating its contemporary use. In this connection, both *ministeriales* and clerics could be burghers in twelfth-century Cologne, if only they held property in the city.

It does not seem proper to me to imagine that *ministerialis* and *burgensis* were mutually exclusive categories. Such an assumption is made by A. Hansay, "L'origine du patriciat à Liège au moyen âge," *RBPH* 2 (1923), p.698. He cites R. Schroeder, *Lehrbuch der deutschen Rechtsge-schichte* 3d ed., p.622: Wer seinen Gerichtsstand nicht vor dem Stadtge-richt hatte, war nicht Bürger. Darum schieden einerseits die Vogtleute der in der Stadt befindlichen Immunitäten . . . unbedingt aus der Bürgerschaft aus, anderseits aber ebenso die Geistlichen und die zu der fürstlichen Hofhaltung gehörigen oder vom Stadtherrn als städtische Beamte (Burg-grafen, Vögte, Schultheissen, Zöllner, Münzmeister und d. gl. m.) verwendeten Ministerialen.

But in twelfth-century Cologne the line is impossible to draw between burghers and urban *ministeriales*. This point, obvious in the sources themselves, is noted by Steinbach, "Zur Sozialgeschichte," p.180, and by Luise von Winterfeld, *Handel, Kapitel, und Patriziat in Köln bis 1400* (Lübeck, 1925). Clerics who possessed real estate in Cologne were also considered bourgeois: cf. Hans Planitz, *Die deutsche Stadt im Mittelalter* (Köln-Graz, 1954), p.256. Full possession of urban property placed one under the city court and made one a burgher. This is recognized even by Hansay, p.700, when he says that some *ministeriales* became burghers by acquiring urban land.

6. Ennen, "The Different Types of Formation," pp.174–82.

merchant gild or the judicial community headed by the urban *scabini*.[7] Neither interpretation is founded on evidence strong enough to command complete agreement, but the judicial community does appear more likely than the merchant gild to have served as the basis for the commune. Both interpretations give scant consideration to the influence of the peace movement, which others have seen, correctly, as an important influence on the development of urban institutions, even if not the source of the commune.

A commune, as it existed in Europe from the end of the eleventh century, was a sworn association that united two distinct principles: a personal or associational principle and a territorial principle.[8] The associational principle may be said to have existed in any group in which the members were pledged to lend one another mutual aid. In most cases the members of such associations shared some common interests, whether they were religious, economic, political, or social, or some combination of these. The usefulness of such associations, even in a society basically established on kinship patterns, is obvious. Religious gilds and other such associations can be shown to have existed in Europe at least by the ninth century. Such an association provided a form of organization to replace the family or sib structure that guaranteed protection and provided various services in a tribe or early

---

7. Hans Planitz, *Die deutsche Stadt im Mittelalter* (Köln-Graz, 1954), is basically a combination of three fundamental articles of his: "Kaufmanns-gilde und städtische Eidgenossenschaft in niederfränkischen Städten im 11. und 12. Jahrhundert," *ZRG* 60 (1940), pp.1—116; "Die Frühgeschichte der deutschen Stadt," *ZRG* 63 (1943), pp.1—91; "Die deutsche Stadtge-meinde," *ZRG* 64 (1944), pp.1—85. The views of Franz Steinbach are included in a series of articles: "Stadtgemeinde und Landgemeinde: Studien zur Geschichte des Bürgertums I," *Rheinische Vierteljahrsblätter* 13 (1948), pp.11—50; *Der Ursprung der Kölner Stadtgemeinde* (Bonn, 1955) [a brief pamphlet] and "Zur Sozialgeschichte von Köln im Mittelalter," *Spiegel der Geschichte: Festgabe für Max Braubach* (Münster, 1964), pp.171—97.
The most basic distinction is whether the *Landgemeinde* (Steinbach) or the *Kaufmannsgilde* (Planitz) is seen as the basis for the urban community, its institutions, and its laws. A review of older theories and an assessment of them is given in Planitz, "Kaufmannsgilde und städtische Eidgenossen-schaft," pp.3—6, and in Gustav Schmoller, *Deutsches Städtewesen in älterer Zeit* (Bonn and Leipzig, 1922), pp.2—32.

8. A concise definition of a commune is given by Henri Pirenne in the article on "Commune, Medieval" in the *Encyclopedia of the Social Sciences* IV (New York, 1931), pp.61—3.

kingdom of the Germanic peoples. Although such associations may occur in less complex societies, as a principle of social organization they are a sign of the growing complexity and interdependence of society. Thus the appearance of both the towns and the associations in the eleventh and twelfth centuries is an indication of the emergence of a more complex society characterized by increasing economic diversity and social mobility.

Medieval urban gilds, especially the merchant gild, embodied the principle of association. The first clear example of a gild of merchants with economic unity as well as the usual social and religious concerns is at Tiel at the beginning of the eleventh century. Probably the most famous of the merchant gilds in the eleventh and twelfth centuries are those at Valenciennes and St. Omer for which important sources are still extant.[9] Cologne had its merchant gild as well. The *praepositus negotiatorum* mentioned in 959 may have been the head of the merchant gild in Cologne. Although not much is known directly about the organization and functions of the merchant gild at Cologne, it continued to exist well into the twelfth century, and some membership lists are still extant.[10] Not surprisingly, the merchant gild disappeared in the twelfth century at the same time that distinctively urban institutions arose. How the Cologne merchant gild may have contributed to the development of an urban community is a subject of dispute, but the associational principle embodied in the gild makes it a possible source for the urban community.

The principal difference between a gild and a commune is what can be termed the principle of territoriality. The commune is also a self-help association, but it applies to all inhabitants of a given area—at least to all those of substance and importance. It is defined in large part as a territorial unit. The commune has definite political responsibility— something which a gild may have only in an incidental sense. The

---

9. Latouche, pp.261–4; Planitz, "Kaufmannsgilde und städtische Eidgenossenschaft," p.27.

10. Lantbert, "Vita Heriberti," *MGH. SS.* IV, p.748. A cleric who was driven by hunger to steal is captured near Cologne "a quodam negoti-atorum preposito" and handed over to the authorities. Edith Ennen, *Frühgeschichte*, p.167, mentions *praepositus negotiatorum* as one of the possible titles for the royally appointed *Wikgraf* or head of the merchant association.

The lists have been published with an interpretation by Heinrich von Loesch, *Die Kölner Kaufmannsgilde im zwölften Jahrhundert* (Trier, 1904).

commune is well suited to become a public organization; the gild only rarely ceases to be a private association.

The territorial principle in Cologne is represented by the court of the *scabini* under the general authority of the *Burggraf* and the *Stadtvogt*. It had a territorial as well as a personal jurisdiction by the twelfth century and had come increasingly under bourgeois control. To be sure, some areas of the city had their own banks of *scabini* and the precise jurisdiction of the *scabini* cannot be fixed; nevertheless, the court of the *scabini*, restricted to the town and a limited area outside the walls (the *Burgbann*), could have formed a partial basis for the urban community, especially its territorial aspect.

One set of institutions, those of the peace associations, combined the associational and the territorial principles. A diocesan peace organization had many of the same characteristics that an urban commune had. Both were sworn associations encompassing everyone in a given territory. Both included to one degree or another the protection of weak persons, the repression of violence, and the protection of certain places (the right of asylum).[11] Those who have studied the peace movement have been unable to find any direct connection between it and the rise of urban communes, but the many similarities that exist between the two different communities do suggest that the peace movement had an indirect influence on the development of urban communes.[12] The first Peace of God that is known in Germany is the *Pax Sigiwini* from the diocese of Cologne in 1083.[13] The *Pax Sigiwini* is typical in most respects. It has characteristics of both a Peace of God and a Truce of

---

11. Albert Vermeesch, *Essai sur les origines et la signification de la commune dans le nord de la France (XIe et XIIe siècles)* (Heule, 1966), pp.85, 138–44. The term *commune* could be applied to a diocesan peace organization; in its most basic sense *commune* seems to have denoted the use of the popular army to enforce the peace (ibid., p.147).

12. Vermeesch, p.175; Luise von Winterfeld, "Gottesfrieden und deutsche Stadtverfassung," *Hansische Geschichtsblätter*, Jahrgang 1927, p.10, n.8, cites Luchaire with approval when he states (Achille Luchaire, *Les communes françaises à l'époque des Capétiens*, 2d ed. (1911), pp.38ff.) that the peace of God was not the basis for the urban commune, but that it did contribute toward the commune's formation, especially because it was a model of the union of association and territoriality. Von Winterfeld's study is an attempt to document this for German cities, especially (almost exclusively) for Cologne.

13. "Pax Sigiwini Archiepiscopi Coloniensis," *MGH. LL.*, Sect. 4 (*Constitutiones*), I, 424; Von Winterfeld, "Gottesfrieden," pp.12–13.

God, including regulations on the bearing of arms and other actions which might affect the peace established in the diocese. There are certain forms of force which do not come under the peace and which are thereby approved, such as constituted authorities carrying out judgments against criminals, a lord punishing a serf, or a master disciplining a scholar. Otherwise all force is outlawed including even the fights of children. As a note of humanitarian interest, children of less than twelve were not to lose a hand for fighting but were only to be reprimanded or whipped.

The archbishop remarks that these regulations were made in consultation with his "parishioners," and the enforcement of them depends on the whole community: "it shall pertain no more to the power and judgment of counts and tribunes and powerful men than to the power and judgment of the whole community to impose the punishments mentioned above on violators of the holy peace."[14] There is no doubt that the community had a responsibility in punishing offenders against the peace, but how that responsibility was to be performed is not indicated. The mutual oath which bound the peace community together appears to be mentioned in one article of the *Pax Sigiwini*.[15]

The *scabini* appear as early leaders of the urban community. The judicial community under their leadership seems the most likely basis for the urban community. The merchant gild and the peace organization contributed to the development of the community, but probably did not provide the basis for it. To support this contention the development of the earliest community in the period 1074–1106 and the tasks undertaken by the new urban regime must be examined. Then the

---

14. "Pax Sigiwini," p.605, art. 15: Non magis in comitum aut tribunorum vel potentum quam in totius communiter populi potestate et arbitrio constabit, ut vindictas superius dictatas violatoribus sanctae pacis inferant. . . .

15. Vermeesch, p.85, emphasizes three elements which the urban communes and the diocesan peace communities had in common: a territorial basis, an oath for self-protection, and a popular army. The territorial basis is clear in the *Pax Sigiwini*. The popular army is not mentioned, though clearly some role is given to the community in enforcing the regulations. The oath for self-protection is not mentioned directly; but it seems to be indirectly indicated in article 13 (ibid., p.605) where a person is to be excommunicated "si . . . huic piae institutioni contraire nititur, ut nec pacem cum aliis Deo promittere nec etiam observare voluerit. . . ."

institutions by which the community was governed can be discussed in detail.

The first united action on the part of the citizens of Cologne—or at least the first of which the annalists and chroniclers took note—occurred in 1074. The bishop of Münster had come to Cologne in that year to celebrate Easter. After the festivities he needed transportation home, and the archbishop of Cologne, ever the obliging host, ordered some of his servants to go to the docks and requisition a boat. The boat they attempted to seize belonged to one of the richest merchants in town, and, to make matters worse, was laden with merchandise. The dock workers objected to this high-handed use of authority, and one of them managed to slip away to tell the merchant what had happened. On hearing the news, the merchant sent his son, some of his workers, and some youths from the city to prevent the seizure of his boat. They succeeded not only in driving away the servants whom the archbishop had sent but also in routing the *Stadtvogt*, who later came to seize the boat.

Tensions between the two sides rose as a result of these events, and the archbishop did not help to reduce them when he threatened to mete out suitable punishment to the seditious youths at the next court session. Eventually the rebels, now joined by more substantial inhabitants of the town, stormed the archbishop's quarters. Barely escaping, he and his followers barricaded themselves in the cathedral. While the townspeople were destroying the archbishop's chapel, they killed an innocent bystander, whom they mistook for the archbishop; he meantime prepared his escape. After dark, he disguised himself and fled from the cathedral by way of the dormitory to the house of a canon who had recently been granted permission to cut a back door out of the town wall. Through this door the archbishop and some companions escaped and rode off into the night to seek help.

After the townspeople discovered that they had been tricked, they set about to defend themselves from the expected counterattack. Meanwhile they found time to execute two persons, including a suspected witch, and to send some youths riding off to convince the king that he should take over the city now that the archbishop had been driven out.

On the fourth day after he had escaped from the city, the archbishop returned with a sizable force he had raised in the neighborhood. The force must have been large, for the burghers sent envoys to meet him, saying that they would surrender to him and submit to any punishment except death. Thus there was no siege, and the archbishop and his forces entered the city unmolested. He compelled the burghers to give him satisfaction, coming before him with bare feet and demonstrating their obedience, but he delayed the judgments against them until the next day.

The archbishop had a difficult problem. The soldiers he had raised in the province wanted revenge and booty, but he managed to persuade many of them to go home. He himself retired outside the city walls to St. Gereon, undoubtedly concerned for his safety in a city that was not yet fully pacified; but he sent an occupation force of his own soldiers into the city to maintain order. Somehow "six hundred of the richest merchants" managed to escape and went off to petition for royal support. On the next day the archbishop's men were given free rein to burn and to loot, and the ringleaders of the rebellion, including the son of the rich merchant, who had started it, were blinded. In addition, the archbishop placed an anathema on the heads of the burghers who had escaped from the city.

The *Annals* of Lambert of Hersfeld are the chief source for the events of 1074.[16] The account is favorable to the archbishop, and some details may well be erroneous; nevertheless, it provides the basis for a number of observations. The most notable information Lambert inadvertently supplies is the weakness of the archbishop within the city.[17] The *Burggraf* is nowhere to be found. If he ever had important military or police functions, he apparently did not exercise them in the late eleventh century. The only official who seems to have been involved in police activity is the *Stadtvogt*, and he apparently could not muster enough support to overcome a few youths and servants. The lack of security in Cologne seems all the stranger since this was the time of the Easter holidays. The archbishop did have a bodyguard, and the church grounds as well as the cathedral had some fortifications that gave him the time to escape; but his forces were not enough to put down the uprising when the more substantial burghers in the city joined the original band of youths and servants. This united force of burghers broke into the churchyard and ultimately had to be let into the cathedral as well. In fact, real military support for the archbishop came only from the countryside. Lambert presents the army raised by the archbishop as a popular uprising, but it appears to have been composed of two parts, the *provinciales* and the *milites* of the archbishop. Those

---

16. Lambert of Hersfeld, "Annales," *MGH. SS.* V, pp.211–5.

17. Koebner, p.108, points this out and makes a number of very useful observations concerning the uprising of 1074.

referred to as *provinciales* may also have stood in a special relationship to the archbishop, but they clearly are regarded as auxiliary or emergency forces. When the city had been surrendered to him, he urged the *provinciales* to return home saying that they had helped him handle the difficult part of the affair and that he could take care of the rest "privately and domestically." He retained the services of his *milites*, however, and sent as many of them into the city as he thought would be necessary to maintain order. It was these same soldiers who carried out the punishments on the following day. Presumably this group included the members of the archbishop's bodyguard and other vassals and *ministeriales* from the countryside, especially from the fortress at Neuss where he had fled when he first was forced to leave Cologne.[18]

Under normal conditions the archbishop apparently relied more on "filial" devotion than on overt force to maintain his lordship in Cologne itself. His paternalistic attitude is amply demonstrated when he requisitioned the boat in the first place. He instructed his servants (*ministri*) to find a suitable boat and simply transfer it into his service (*in ministerium archiepiscopi expedire*). This same paternalistic attitude is evident in the notion that the punishment was something to be settled "domestically and privately." However lordship may have expressed itself legally, this was the sort of attitude that was galling to the burghers in 1074 and from which they freed themselves in the course of the twelfth and thirteenth centuries.

Lambert's account also gives us some insight into the town community in the latter half of the eleventh century. He equates townspeople with merchants and artisans; in his account, nonmercantile landowners and urban *ministeriales* do not appear. The original incident was mercantile, and, when the six hundred burghers flee Cologne to plan yet more dastardly deeds, they are described as six hundred market-men (*mercatores*). Furthermore, Lambert delights in contrasting the thriving city before the uprising, whose bustling streets could hardly hold the crowds, with the deserted city afterwards, where a man was seldom seen.[19] It is obvious from other sources that nonmercantile elements

---

18. In the charters of the eleventh and twelfth centuries the *ministeriales* are seldom if ever listed as *milites*; nevertheless, it is obvious that the archbishop's *ministeriales* formed an important element in the force of 1074. Lambert apparently does not intend the word *milites* in any social or technical sense.

19. Lambert, "Annales," *MGH. SS.* V, p.215: Ita civitas paulo ante civibus frequentissima et post Mogontiam caput et princeps Gallicarum urbium, subito pene redacta est in solitudinem; et cuius plateae vix

existed in the city, but the emphasis Lambert gives is significant. Cologne was first and foremost a mercantile city whose long-distance traders gave it its dominant tone.

The background and the influence of a rich merchant of the time are also clearly shown. Lambert is scornful of city life, yet attracted to it. Cologne was a place where all one's desires could be gratified, where every sort of pleasure could be sought. He sneers especially at the easy life of the burghers, who have been brought up in the delights of the city. Such men, he says, after a day of buying and selling, like to sit around over wine and idly discuss military affairs; and it is all the easier for them to do so because they have no experience in military matters.[20] The resistance of the burghers in 1074 and their rather startling success in 1106, which will be discussed later, make Lambert's contempt for the fighting capabilities of the burghers appear rather exaggerated. But the most important conclusion that can be drawn from Lambert's comments is that Cologne was a well-established mercantile center by 1074. The city dwellers have been raised in the city from birth. They appear to be sedentary and, in many cases, rich.

The merchant whose boat was seized was one of the most substantial citizens of Cologne, a group Lambert refers to as the *primores*. These *primores* came together after the initial incident and decided that they should join the rebellion. According to a few historians, this shows that a commune was already in existence in Cologne in 1074. This conclusion is scarcely necessary since all Lambert says is that the *primores* conferred and made some bad decisions (*conferunt primores inepta consilia*). The uprising appears to have been spontaneous, and there is no indication in Lambert's account of fixed institutional procedures among the burghers. Yet it would be a mistake to overlook the degree of cooperation present among the burghers. It was undoubtedly based on the two things that did the most to hold the medieval town together—a community of economic interest and family alliances. One can easily imagine the outrage of the *primores*, if they were

---

capiebant stipata viantium examina, nunc rarum ostendit hominem, silentio et horrore omnia desiderii quondam ac deliciarum loca possidentibus.

20. Ibid., p.212: Nec difficile fuit, id hominum genus in omne quod velles, tamquam folium quod vento rapitur, transformare, quippe qui ab ineunte aetate inter urbanas delicias educati, nullam in bellicis rebus experientiam habebant, quique post venditas merces inter vina et epulas de re militari disputare soliti, omnia quae animo occurrissent tam facilia factu quam dictu putabant, exitus rerum metiri nesciebant.

merchants, when the boat of a fellow merchant was seized. Although Lambert nowhere mentions it, the Cologne merchant gild may well have taken action here. Furthermore, family connections were important. Lambert describes the youth who initiated the revolt, the son of the rich merchant, as "a young man who excelled no less in boldness than in strength and who was well-liked by the *primores* partly because of his accomplishments and partly because of his family connections."[21] The existence of a certain elite in the city (the *primores*) is indicated, a kind of community based on similar economic interests and family connections, the basis on which a medieval patriciate could be built.

This rich, sedentary merchant of Cologne also had a group of workers who were loyal to him. These *famuli* may not have been personally dependent on him (although it is difficult to believe that *famuli* would not arouse connotations of *familia*, and in the thirteenth century some patricians of Cologne were accused of having *Muntmanni*)[22] but they were loyal enough at least to run to him when they were told to hand the boat over and to fight with his son in the first stage of the rebellion. Altogether, the picture is one of a rich, well-connected merchant living with a sizable staff in a well-established community.

Lambert also suggests a larger context into which the events of 1074 in Cologne can be placed. He says that the burghers of Cologne did not want to seem less worthy than those of Worms, who a short time before had driven their bishop from the city and appealed to the king to occupy it. Henry IV was in a particularly bad position in 1073–74. Most of the princes, both secular and ecclesiastical, had turned against him; and some were even calling for his deposition. The revolt in Worms in 1073 was a turning point in his fortunes. The ecclesiastical princes, especially, felt it necessary to make some accommodation with the king in order to protect themselves in their cities.[23] It was this revolt, Lambert says, that the inhabitants of Cologne were imitating. For this reason they sent some intrepid youths riding off to get royal support at the height of the conflict, and for the same reason the six hundred

---

21. Ibid., p.212: ... filium ... non minus audacia quam viribus excellentem, et tum propter generis affinitatem tum ob merita sua primoribus civitatis maxime carum et acceptum.

22. They were accused of this by the archbishop in the Great Arbitration of 1258: Lacomblet II 452, article 19 (p.245).

23. Karl Hampe, *Deutsche Kaisergeschichte in der Zeit der Salier und Staufer*, revised by Friederich Baethgen, 11. Auflage (Heidelberg, 1963), pp.47–8.

mercatores who fled went to the king to seek his aid. The emergence of the Rhenish bourgeoisie as a factor in imperial politics is clear in the 1070's, even though it was more important potentially than actually. The inhabitants of Worms received some toll privileges from the grateful king; the inhabitants of Cologne were put down by their archbishop. If the king intervened after the uprising had been quashed, it benefited only his political position, not the status of the burghers.[24] Good relations between the burghers and the king continued because they both had an interest in controlling the archbishop and their interests could and did coincide at times. More than this, however, the burghers of Cologne seem to have felt a genuine affection for Henry IV, as their actions in 1106 demonstrate.

There is no evidence that the uprising of 1074 gave rise to an urban government or a commune in Cologne; however, after 1106, it is undeniable that some sort of urban regime existed. During the revolt in 1106 the burghers undertook communal tasks, especially in building and maintaining fortifications, that could only have been borne by a regular communal regime. The evidence for a commune, in a strict sense, as a community of inhabitants of a given area who swore an oath of mutual protection, is, as we shall see, rather meager; but after 1106 some sort of community organization with a degree of autonomy from the archbishop must have existed.

Henry IV had been deprived of the empire by his son Henry V in 1105. In the early spring of 1106, in a desperate attempt to regain political leadership, he fled to the northwestern part of the empire and enlisted the support of the bishop and burghers of Liége, the duke of Lower Lorraine, and the burghers of Cologne, among others. After he and his followers had checked Henry V's army in a battle on the Meuse and had celebrated Easter in Liége, Henry returned to Cologne and extracted an oath from the citizens that they would fortify the city and

---

24. Luise von Winterfeld in her article "Neue Untersuchungen über die Anfänge des Gemeinwesens der Stadt Köln," *VSWG* 18 (1924–25), p.12, says that the king came to the aid of the city immediately after the burghers escaped and appealed for his help. Then the king is supposed to have sat in stern judgment over the archbishop for a long time before the two were reconciled for political reasons. She does not give the source for these statements. In fact, she seems to indicate that they are based on Lambert's account, but Lambert does not mention any intervention on the part of the king. In any case, the burghers gained nothing from the trial; however, it may be that the king earned the affection that he obviously enjoyed among the burghers of Cologne through some such intervention.

defend it for him. The inhabitants of Cologne not only strengthened the existing walls, but added ditches and earthworks around three suburbs, Niederich, Airsbach, and Holy Apostles. This is the first sure indication that exists of cooperation between the old city, which of course had included the mercantile quarter of St. Martin since the tenth century, and the suburbs. Both Niederich, called the *burgum inferius*, and Airsbach, called the *burgum superius* (also *Overburg*), had a rather dense population, including artisans and merchants; but Holy Apostles was sparsely populated, and the land there was devoted mainly to agriculture.

According to the *Annals of Hildesheim* the fortifications were undertaken following plans suggested by Henry IV himself, and they served their purpose. Shortly after the feast of St. Peter and St. Paul, Henry V besieged Cologne with a substantial army. The heat of the summer, the fortifications, and the bravery of the burghers of Cologne (who fought "like brave soldiers . . . the like of which had never before been seen," the monk of Hildesheim concedes) proved too much for Henry V; he lifted the siege after three weeks and withdrew to Aachen.

The death of Henry IV towards the end of the summer altered the situation radically. The bishop of Liége made his peace with Henry V, and the only two opponents of the king left in the northwest were Henry, the duke of Lower Lorraine, who was eventually deprived of his duchy, and the burghers of Cologne. Henry V was determined to take revenge on Cologne and called together another army, as well as a fleet of boats to assault Cologne from the river. The burghers naturally hastened to make peace with him and eventually bought him off for a considerable amount of silver.[25]

Despite their ultimate military failure, the burghers of Cologne now had established common tasks, which required common government. The defense of the city was not very effective under the archbishop's lordship in the later eleventh century, as the events of 1074 show. In fact, the initial success of the burghers then may well have been possible because they were the ones already responsible for Cologne's defense. In any event, after 1106 there is little doubt that military leadership in matters of defense and financial authority in order to maintain the fortifications were necessary. That the urban community assumed these tasks is shown clearly in the course of the twelfth century.

The abbey of St. Trond had three houses in Cologne, one of which was part of the urban fortifications facing the Rhine. Sometime between

25. The most important source for the events of 1106 are the "Annales Hildesheimenses," *MGH. SS.* III, pp. 110–1.

1108 and 1136 this house was held by a certain Berner, who owed the abbot one-half mark a year and rights of hospitality for it. In addition, Berner had to keep the fortifications of the house in good repair and provide military service in the event of siege. The cost of any repairs and that of hiring men to defend the house was to be borne in the ratio of one third by Berner and two thirds by the abbey. In 1177 the abbot of St. Trond granted the house to Heinrich Saphir, an important twelfth-century burgher, and his wife. Heinrich owed six marks rent a year and rights of hospitality. The costs of further building or repair were to be borne by Heinrich alone, although he was exempt from the payment of the rent for four years if the house were destroyed. Finally, Heinrich was to provide the military service required from the property if the city of Cologne were engaged in a war. The abbot of St. Trond, then, arranged to have the military obligation on the abbey's property discharged by Berner and by Heinrich Saphir; the charge lay on the house not on the men as members of a commune.[26]

In 1154 the inhabitants of the area dependent on St. Pantaleon were expressly exempted by the archbishop from the payment of certain city taxes unless they were included within the city walls at some later date. The common task of defense and the city taxes were clearly recognized as interdependent.[27] The jurisdiction of the urban court (the *Burgbann*)

---

26. For Berner: "Gesta Abbatum Trudonensium," *MGH. SS.* X, p.288. These are the most important passages: Tertia vero domus, quoniam una est de capitalibus turribus urbis Coloniae, si forte obsessa fuerit urbs, hoc ei per nos debet, ut custodibus nostris et stipendio muniatur et defendatur, cavendumque nobis est, sicut eam diligimus, ut pro maceria et tectura ruinam nullam patiatur.... Ego vero ad hoc postea hospitem nostrum in ea Bernerum perduxi, ut tam ipse quam omnes qui post eum in ea vellent manere, si forte urbs obsideretur, aut domus aliquam ruinam minaretur aut defectus reparandos pateretur, omnem tertiam partem constitutarum solverent, et tertium hominem pro defendenda urbe in ea ponerent et stipendiarent, dimidiam vero marcam non minus solverent.

For Heinrich Saphir: H. I, p.163 (Martin 11 II 1). For Heinrich these arrangements were summed up: Si civitas Coloniensis aliqua werra laboraverit, castrensis milicie debitum eciam providebunt.

27. Lacomblet I 67: This document is interesting for a number of reasons, especially for the clear connection it presents between defense and taxation and for the evidence it offers of local rights held by the inhabitants of St. Pantaleon before inclusion in the commune: ... Igitur cum aduersus habitatores uille s. Pantaleonis uerbum exactionis crebro moueretur, ut ad communem ciuium collectam ipsi pro parte sua

extended beyond the city walls, but the taxes were dependent on the common task of fortification, not on the judicial authority. By the provisions of the privileges of St. Pantaleon confirmed in 1154, the people who lived there must have started paying city taxes in 1180. While Archbishop Philip was engaged in the struggle against Henry the Lion, for which he received the duchy of Westphalia and Engern,[28] the burghers of Cologne undertook a very ambitious defense project. They built a ring of fortifications, later replaced by a stone wall, around Cologne including the suburbs of St. Pantaleon, St. Severin, and St. Gereon, which lay outside the old walls. This is the medieval wall of Cologne and represents the farthest extension of the fortifications in the medieval period. The area they included in this widening of the city was for the most part sparsely settled agricultural land, dependent on one of the ecclesiastical foundations in the area in one way or another, but much of it was held by burghers in the twelfth century.

The process by which the widening of the city was accomplished is not clear. Surely some sort of understanding with the heads of the ecclesiastical foundations would have been necessary as was an understanding with the archbishop, who was after all still lord of the city. It is nevertheless significant that this ambitious project was undertaken peacefully and with a minimum of friction between the burghers and the archbishop. He demanded that the citizens of Cologne pay him a lump sum of 2,000 marks for infringing on his rights. In addition to the fortifications, certain buildings had been erected illegally on public land on the banks of the Rhine, in the market area, and in other public places without the archbishop's consent. He allowed the buildings to remain too,

---

cooperarentur et darent, illi uero de nullo iure hoc se debere antiqua et probabili ueritate confirmarent, uerbum hoc, quia de facili non poterat terminari, ad nostram perlatum est audientiam. Veritate igitur diligenter indagata et cognita inuenimus, eos ab antiquo fuisse et esse liberos et absolutos tam a debito thelonei, quam ab omni eiusmodi ciuilium collectarum exactione. Proinde deum et ueritatem intuentes memorate uille s. Pantaleonis et eius habitatoribus uniuersis, qui eorum uicinie iure tenentur, sue libertatis et absolutionis iusticiam hactenus habitam nostra auctoritate et ciuium consensu in omne posterum integre concedimus . . . hoc apponente, si quandoque uallo et muro ciuibus coadunentur, communi etiam ciuium iure teneantur. Si quis uero intra muros mansionem et proprietatem habens eiusmodi absolutionis occasione ad ipsos se transferat, ipsum a nostre pagine constitutione secludimus.

28. The disposition of the lands of Henry the Lion at the Diet of Würzburg in 1180 appears in *MGH. LL*. Sect. 4 (*Constitutiones*) I, p.385.

but demanded a yearly payment from each of them, two *nummi* for a small area, four *nummi* for a large one.[29] But, most importantly, he gave his consent after the fact to a project undertaken wholly on bourgeois initiative. In fact, the provision of the privileges for St. Pantaleon in 1154 that says the inhabitants there shall not pay city taxes unless they are included at some future time within the city walls almost seems to suggest that the widening of the walls was regarded as natural and inevitable. These events in 1180 demonstrate most forcefully the character of relations between the archbishop and the town in the twelfth century. Between the period of the great uprisings (1074, 1106) and the bitter struggle for control of the town in the thirteenth century, relative calm prevailed. Yet the twelfth century is precisely the period in which urban institutions underwent their most profound transformation; it is precisely the period when the foundations of the independence of Cologne were laid.

The urban government of Cologne held considerable property in the twelfth century. The city hall was located in St. Lawrence parish. This is surprising since St. Lawrence was the parish adjacent to the archbishop's palace, the parish in which the Jewish quarter was located, and the one area where nonurban *ministeriales* held substantial amounts of land. It would seem more natural for the city hall to have been located in the mercantile quarter, the parish of St. Martin; but, as we shall see, the supposed opposition between mercantile and older lordship elements is not very clear-cut in Cologne in the twelfth century. However strange the location of the city hall may seem, it is clearly an example of property held by the community. Other examples occur in the agreement with Archbishop Philip in 1180 mentioned above and in a letter to Pope Honorius III from about 1218. In 1180 Philip demanded that certain buildings in the old market, which up to that time had been held by the parishes of St. Martin, St. Brigida, and Airsbach without hereditary right, be transferred to the community of the whole town. The community was to hold the property by hereditary right in return for payments to the archbishop.[30] In 1218 the city of Cologne wrote to

---

29. *Quellen* I 94. A *nummus* was apparently a penny. Cf. Lacomblet 403 (1160), where some properties pay *solidi*, others *nummi*.

30. Ibid.: Adjectum est autem, ut edificia, que in veteri foro parrochiani sancti Martini et parrochiani sancte Brigide et illi de oversburg absque iure hereditario hactenus tenuerunt, universitati ciuium hereditario iure possidenda conferrent.

To my knowledge, this is the only twelfth-century reference to the urban community as a *universitas civium*.

Honorius III concerning a hospital which had been endowed by Heinrich Halverogge, a citizen of Cologne, in the parish of St. Severin. The authorities of Cologne had endowed an oratory at the hospital and established a priest who could minister to the sick and dying; however, the deacon and chapter of St. Severin had tried to prevent this, insisting that divine services and burial must take place in the parish church of St. Severin. Eventually the deacon and chapter were persuaded with a little money to allow the oratory to remain at the hospital. For our purposes, the interesting aspect of these events is that the authorities of Cologne endowed the oratory with a piece of land that was at their disposal for public use.[31] Thus community government in Cologne in the twelfth century was responsible for fortification, could collect taxes to support such enterprises, and held land for common or public purposes.

The *ius coloniensis*, the urban law that pertained to the city as a whole, is mentioned frequently in the twelfth century. Besides belonging to the city community, an inhabitant of Cologne belonged to a parish community. Thus there was also a parish law in each of the parishes. The term *cives* can refer either to the urban community (*Gesamtgemeinde*) or to the parish communities (*Sondergemeinden*). As we shall see, the way in which the *Sondergemeinden* of the old city were related historically to the *Gesamtgemeinde* is still a debatable question; however, the example of St. Pantaleon shows the preexistence of local communities in the outlying regions of Cologne in the twelfth century. In 1154 when the archbishop declared the inhabitants of St. Pantaleon free from city taxes, he described them as being bound by the *ius vicinie* of St. Pantaleon. This *ius* applied to the inhabitants of St. Pantaleon, but it could also apparently be acquired by persons outside the *villa* of St. Pantaleon if they transferred property to the church. The archbishop explicitly forbade those who lived within the walls of Cologne from trying to escape city taxes by transferring their property to St. Pantaleon. The existence of urban law and rights as distinct from parish law and rights is also clearly indicated in this document of 1154 when the archbishop said that, if St. Pantaleon were included within the city walls, the inhabitants should be bound by the city laws.[32]

Although St. Pantaleon was not under urban law in 1154, the *villa* of Marsdorf, which was farther from Cologne but still within the *Burgbann*,

---

31. *Quellen* II 60: ... Nos quidem decorem dei ampliare cupientes, fundum quendam ad nostrum usum publicum spectantem dicto hospitali in subsidium contulimus adiuvamen. . . .

32. Lacomblet I 67. See above, n.27.

apparently was under the law of Cologne. In 1159 the collegial church of St. Gereon, which at that time lay just outside the walls of Cologne, as did St. Pantaleon, purchased some allodial land in Marsdorf. The transaction was made according to the urban law of Cologne through city officials.[33] Of course, the aspects of urban law involved in St. Pantaleon in 1154 and in Marsdorf in 1159 are quite different. One concerns fortifications, the other land transfer. Probably the inhabitants of Marsdorf did not pay for the upkeep of the city walls either since Marsdorf was never included within the city walls.

No reference to the *ius coloniensis* antedates the twelfth century. One of the earliest references is to a Cologne woman named Wendichen, who was described by the abbot of St. Martin in a document of 1142 as a Cologne citizen who was born under urban law.[34] But by 1180 the rights of Cologne citizens were explicitly confirmed by Archbishop Philip in the often mentioned document concerning fortifications. He wanted to avoid further dissension, he said, so he recognized "all the rights of the citizens and the city as well as all good and reasonable customs that the burghers are known to have had either inside or outside the city up to the composition of this document."[35] He did not indicate what these "rights" and "customs" were, but with the inclusion of both categories, those rights more or less formally granted and those that developed through custom, he put the archiepiscopal seal of approval on the very important development of urban law in the twelfth century.

The existence of an urban community in Cologne in the twelfth century, with common duties, common property, and common law, is undeniable. The evidence for the actual foundation of a commune is much weaker. The one bit of evidence which is usually adduced as proof that a formally constituted commune existed in Cologne in the twelfth century is an entry in the *Annals of Cologne* (the *chronica regia* or *Annales Maximi* of Cologne) under the year 1112. About one hundred years after the year of the entry, a monk of St. Pantaleon in composing

33. Lacomblet I 74: Ipsa . . . facta est legitimo donationis modo, secundum ius coloniensis urbis per ipsos iudices colonienses, sub presentia senatorum et ciuium. . . .

34. *Quellen* I 51: . . . quedam wendichin ciuis coloniensis et sub iure et lege ciuili a primeuis parentibus exorta. . . .

35. *Quellen* I 94: Et ne qua recidiue contentionis et discordie prebeatur occasio, omnia iura ciuium et ciuitatis nec non et omnes bonas et rationabiles consuetudines, quas uel intra uel extra ciuitatem burgenses usque ad confectionem presentis carte habuisse noscuntur.

the annals placed the following entry under 1112: *Conjuratio Coloniae facta est pro libertate*.[36] Nothing further is said about it; the sentence stands laconic and alone. It is possible, of course, that it does refer to the formation of a commune by the burghers of Cologne in 1112. But nothing is known about 1112; therefore, it is usual to assume that the entry of 1112 means that the archbishop recognized an urban commune which had already been formed in 1106.[37] Why this sentence should be construed as archiepiscopal recognition is not at all clear except that such a construction has the advantage of allowing us to bridge the gap between 1106, a year well suited to the formation of a commune, and 1112, the year under which the entry appears. The most important word in the sentence is *conjuratio*. It is difficult not to equate the word with *commune*, yet it is not necessary to do so. The word is not used in a technical sense. *Conjurationes* were common occurrences in the twelfth century, and they by no means always designate urban communes. For example, in 1159 the *ministeriales* of Utrecht formed a *conjuratio* against their bishop. They received support from the other "citizens" of the town, but it was clearly a revolt instigated by the *ministeriales* "in order to preserve their rights."[38] There is no indication

---

36. "Annales Colonienses Maximi: Recensio II," *MGH. SS.* XVII, p.749.

37. This, at least, is the opinion of Planitz, "Kaufmannsgilde und städtische Eidgenossenschaft," p.64. In what sense this "recognition" is meant is not clear. Koebner, pp.339–41, argues that a *conjuratio* as an external form of the communal development was missing in Cologne (p.341: Sie [the burghers of Cologne] konnten ein verbrieftes Freiheitsrecht ebenso entbehren, wie sie die Schwurvereinigung als äussere Form der Gemeinschaftsverfassung fallen lassen konnten.). Koebner points out that acquisition of bourgeois status was not dependent on entry into a *Schwurverband* and that a council of *jurati* did not come into being at this time. Luise von Winterfeld, in an article which is really a penetrating critique of Koebner's book, "Neue Untersuchungen," *VSWG* 18 (1924–25), p.9, takes Koebner to task for denying that it was necessary to swear an oath in the twelfth century. She does not, however, consider the predominant territorial emphasis of the twelfth-century evidence we do have.

38. "Annales Egmundani," *MGH. SS.* XVI, p.461: Eodem anno (1159) ministeriales Traiectenses fortissima conjuratione in invicem ad conservandum ius suum coniuraverunt. . . . Egressus (the bishop) autem adversus omnes cives Traiectenses et ecclesiae ministeriales in iram exarsit. . . .
It is interesting that this conflict was settled through the mediation of Rainald of Dassel, Archbishop of Cologne.

that a commune was formed. Or again, in the confused situation in
1106, the bishop of Münster faced a *conjuratio* of his *ministeriales*, who
were assisted by the Count of Westphalia; they even handed him over to
the partisans of Henry IV.[39] Thus *conjuratio* cannot be considered a
technical term that always indicates an urban commune.

The use of the word *Coloniae* is also not as unambiguous as it might
at first appear. The term *Colonienses,* which is, if anything, more
specific than *Coloniae*, was applied in a number of ways in the twelfth
century. It could refer to the inhabitants of the *civitas* in the narrow
sense, as those within the *Burgbann* (or, alternatively, within the walls)
of Cologne; or it could refer to the inhabitants of the *civitas* in the
wider sense, as those within the diocese, or even as those who were
dependent on or partisans of the archbishop of Cologne. Thus, in the
same annals that mention the *conjuratio* of 1112, *Colonienses* are
mentioned in Frisian and Saxon campaigns in the years 1113 and 1114.
These are clearly lords and knights from the diocese of Cologne, not the
burghers of Cologne, as has sometimes been assumed.[40] *Coloniae* need
not refer to the burghers in 1112 any more than *Colonienses* in the
years following.

Even if the *conjuratio* is assumed to have been sworn by the burghers
in 1112, there is no indication that it was a lasting institution. There is
the reference to the *universitas civium* in 1180;[41] there was conceived
to be, then, a body that bore the vested rights of the burghers. But the
memory of the *conjuratio* as an act of foundation was lost. No further
mention of it is made in the twelfth century, and Gottfried Hagen,

---

39. "Annales Colonienses Maximi: Recensio I," *MGH. SS*. XVII, p.745:
Burchardus Monasteriensis episcopus, conjurantibus adversus eum ecclesiae
ministerialibus, annitente comite Westfaliae, ad imperatorem ducitur, in
vincula conicitur.

40. Ibid., pp.749–51. Koebner, pp.271–6, exaggerates the role of the
burghers of Cologne in the wars of 1113–4. They probably helped in the
defense of Deutz, but for the most part references to *Colonienses* in the
annals do not indicate the burghers. For example, the following entry
appears in "Recensio I" under the year 1114: Cum autem reverteretur
(Henry V), Colonienses irruunt in eum viriliter quidem, sed inutiliter.
Capti enim sunt ibi ex eorum melioribus comes Gerardus de Gulike,
Lambertus de Mulenarke. . . . The count of Jülich and the lord of
Mulenark were not Cologne Burghers! Koebner also exaggerates the
freedom in "diplomacy" the Cologne burghers supposedly enjoyed in this
period.

41. *Quellen* I 94. See above, n.30.

writing about the history of Cologne in the thirteenth century, writes as if the patrician regime that existed then were of Roman origin.

Despite the weakness of the reference from 1112 as evidence for the formation of a commune, it is probable that some sort of association was formed. Yet what is striking about the twelfth-century evidence is the predominance of the territorial or real element over the associational or personal element. The basis for membership in the town community was the holding of property in the town. An example of this on the parish level is given by the laws and regulations of Niederich. There it is stated that "for anyone who shall have acquired any hereditary property in our parish and shall have paid us our due, it is our (duty) to come to his aid and defend him against any accuser."[42] There is no word here of an oath as a prerequisite for membership in the parish community, only the acquisition of property and the registration of it with the parish officials. There is no sure evidence of an oath for membership in the city community, either, until the 1280's.[43] It is usually assumed that such an oath existed because there were groups in the town who were clearly not burghers, but these were poorer men who did not have property. One of the unusual aspects of communal life in Cologne in the twelfth century is that clerics held bourgeois land.[44] An early example of this is the property of the abbot of St. Trond mentioned above.[45] Clearly the real element is more important than the personal element in this case. The charge rests not on the abbot as a member of the bourgeois commune, if this is conceived principally as a sworn association, but on the urban land held incidentally by the abbot. The territorial element is predominant in these examples. But, if the commune is assumed to have begun as an association of merchants, they

---

42. *Das Niedericher Weistum* printed in Konrad Beyerle, "Die Anfänge des Kölner Schreinwesens," *ZRG* 51 (1931), pp.501–3. Article 7 (p.502): Quicunque vero hereditatem aliquam inter nos comparaverit et nobis iura nostra persolverit, nostrum est, illi succurrere et defendere contra quemlibet impetentem.

The paying of "iura nostra" evidently refers to the fees for the registration of the property transaction.

43. Even von Winterfeld, "Neue Untersuchungen," p.9, admits this.

44. Philippe Dollinger, "Les Villes allemandes au moyen âge: les groupements sociaux," *La Ville* II (Brussels, 1955), p.378; Koebner, p.446.

45. H. I, p.163. See above, n.26.

transformed this association into an entity with territorial inclusiveness and political leadership with remarkable rapidity.

All of this is not sufficient to prove that a sworn commune did not exist in the twelfth century (it is virtually impossible to prove the nonexistence of something) but it does indicate that private associational ties should not be emphasized to the detriment of other relationships. The reference in 1112 cannot be taken as convincing proof that a commune was formally constituted; still less can it be taken as the source of all urban institutions and urban law. It is well to remember that those who rely heavily on the "events" of 1112 are leaning on a very weak reed.

But if the burghers of Cologne did not form a sworn commune or some sort of conspiratorial secret society, how were they able to erode the power of the archbishop in the town? The archbishop's position in the empire and his consequent inattention to urban affairs provide a partial answer. The archbishops of Cologne were important figures in the twelfth-century empire. They had the right to crown the new German king, although this was disputed by Mainz occasionally. Lothair of Supplinburg was crowned by Archbishop Frederick in 1125, Frederick I by Archbishop Arnold in 1152, Henry VI by Archbishop Philip in 1169, and both Otto of Brunswick (1198) and Philip of Swabia (1204) by Archbishop Adolf.[46] They were also the imperial archchancellors for Italy since 1031, but this title was largely honorary. Much more important, several of them had been imperial chancellors before their elevation to the archiepiscopal see, and they remained directly active in the emperor's campaigns and diplomacy even after they had assumed their new office. Three of ten twelfth-century archbishops of Cologne had been chancellors: Arnold II of Wied (1151–56), Rainald of Dassel (1159–67), and Philip of Heinsberg (1167–91).[47] The other twelfth-century archbishops were active in imperial politics as well, especially in Italy. Bruno II died in Bari in 1137; Hugo was selected to succeed him, but died the same year, without ever leaving Italy. Frederick died near Pavia in 1158.[48]

The most striking example of an archbishop who was nearly always absent from Cologne was Rainald of Dassel. Emperor Frederick I set out

46. The following material on the archbishops is based primarily on the "Annales Colonienses Maximi," *MGH. SS.* XVII.

47. H. I, p.251 (Laur. 4 III 6: 1170–82); *Quellen* I 85 (1174); Friedrich-Wilhelm Oediger, *Geschichte des Erzbistums Köln* I (Köln, 1964), pp.180, 220–1, 228–9, 230–2.

48. Oediger, pp.217, 222.

on his second, and most successful, Italian expedition in 1158. With him was Rainald of Dassel, his chancellor, who had been a party to the famous dispute over *beneficia* at Besançon with the papal legates the previous year. The new archbishop of Cologne, Frederick II, whose election was disputed, had followed the emperor to Nürnberg and Regensburg, where he finally got the emperor's approval. Then the new archbishop proceeded to Rome for the pope's blessing and the *pallium*. He had joined Frederick's forces when he suddenly died of one of those diseases that plagued German armies in Italy. Frederick I sent messengers bearing letters to Cologne, instructing them to elect Rainald as Archbishop Frederick's successor. Rainald was duly elected although he remained in Italy, where his services were still very much needed.[49]

Rainald did arrive in Cologne in 1159, but his mission was to raise more troops for the Italian wars; he did not have time to be installed as archbishop. He returned to Italy with the fresh troops and did not come back to Cologne until 1165, when the Italian affairs had been brought under control. There had been a serious disturbance in his lands in the previous year, when the emperor's brother, the count palatine Conrad, had attempted to take the fortress at Rheineck. Rainald resisted this encroachment without ever leaving Italy, relying on his local vassals and allies, who mobilized enough men to make Conrad back down. When Rainald and the emperor returned to Germany in 1165, Rainald had to answer Conrad's charges in an imperial court, which he successfully did. The grand year of Rainald's direct association with Cologne was 1165. He returned to Cologne with the bones of the Wise Men, which were part of the booty from the destruction of Milan. No single act of religious devotion in the history of medieval Cologne was as magnificent as this delivery of stolen relics. Finally, six years after his election, Rainald was elevated to the priesthood and consecrated as archbishop with the emperor and empress in attendance. But the very next year he was off on another Italian expedition, one from which he never returned. Twice he had been in Cologne; once briefly to raise troops and once grandly to be installed in his office. For the rest of his reign, he was still what he had been before 1159, the emperor's chief agent.

Admittedly Rainald's career as archbishop was exceptional. None of the other twelfth-century archbishops was absent for so much of his reign or so preoccupied with imperial affairs. Philip of Heinsberg, Rainald's successor, was also elected while in Italy in 1168, but he

---

49. Oediger, p.223; on Rainald, see Walther Föhl, "Studien zu Rainald von Dassel," *Jahrbuch des kölnischen Geschichtvereins* 17 (1935), pp.234–59, 20 (1938), pp.238–60.

returned to Cologne the same year, and remained more involved in Germany than in Italy. Frederick I relied on Archbishop Christian of Mainz, another chancellor who had been rewarded with an archiepiscopal see, for Italian affairs in this period. Philip did take part in the disastrous Italian expeditions in the 1170's. He went with Frederick in 1174, was sent back to Germany to raise fresh troops in 1176 and was present at the Peace of Venice in 1178. Then, at his death in 1191, he was with Henry VI in Apulia. But in the meantime, his primary interests lay in Germany.[50]

Philip's policies in Germany were sometimes in accord with the emperor's policies and sometimes not. Philip was more keenly aware of the possibilities of expanding his local overlordship than his predecessors had been. Both he and Rainald of Dassel had sought to extend their control on the right bank of the Rhine. Philip spearheaded Frederick I's campaign against Henry the Lion and received the duchy of Westphalia and Engern as a reward. Much of his reign was devoted to impressing Cologne's presence on the newly acquired Saxon territories. Philip strengthened Soest, building a new palace and new walls, large enough to enclose six parishes. He brought more and more powerful lords into the vassalage of the archbishop by purchasing important properties and giving them back to the original owners as fiefs. In the process he depleted the financial resources of the archbishop to such an extent that his successors were often seriously in debt. Philip's vigorous policy of aggrandizement also led him into conflict with the emperor he had previously served; however, Philip was restored to favor at Mainz in 1188. When news of Frederick I's death reached the West, Philip fought for Henry VI's interests against the Landgrave of Thuringia and then proceeded to Italy to join the new emperor in his campaign in Apulia, where he died.[51]

The absence of the archbishop from Cologne was an important factor in the peaceful development of the urban community. As noted in the discussion of the upheaval of 1074, the archbishop did not have an elaborate administration to govern Cologne in his absence; he had to rely on bourgeois groups themselves to control an increasingly complex society. There is little indication in the twelfth century that he had any doubts about this state of affairs. Archbishop Philip had strengthened

---

50. Oediger, pp.230ff.

51. I have been unable to consult H. Hecker, *Die territoriale Politik des Erzbischofs Philip I. von Köln* (Leipzig, 1883), but a useful discussion is included in Hermann Rothert, *Westfälische Geschichte* I, 2d ed. (Gütersloh, 1962), pp.182–92.

the fortifications of Soest on his own initiative; he had no reason to complain if the burghers strengthened the fortifications at Cologne on their own initiative, as they did in 1180, as long as they respected his rights and acknowledged his leadership. The archbishop and the burghers probably did cooperate to some degree in the development of urban institutions in Cologne. It would be a mistake to imagine that the archbishop was always implacably opposed to the innovations introduced. There is no evidence that relations between the archbishop and the town were strained at any time in the course of the twelfth century after 1106, except in 1138–9 and, perhaps, in 1180, when the potentially explosive issue of defense and fortification was settled amicably.[52] But, if the evidence indicates little open conflict, it does not indicate very many instances of active cooperation. The archbishop's policy towards the town might better be summed up as one of salutary neglect. He was too involved in Lombardy or in Westphalia to concern himself much with affairs in Cologne. He does not seem to have assumed that the internal development in Cologne posed a threat to his lordship and his territorial ambitions.

It should not be surprising, then, that the development of the urban community in Cologne in the twelfth century lacks the color and the fire of an operatic second act. Oaths of unrelenting vengeance or conspiratorial machinations are out of place. An urban community did develop after 1106, but with the archbishop's sufferance if not his cooperation. The later conflicts between the town and the archbishop arose at least in part from the particular way in which urban institutions developed in the twelfth century, and these institutions must be discussed in detail.

---

52. The dispute with Archbishop Arnold I arose in 1138, the year of his election to the see. "Annales Colonienses Maximi," *MGH. SS.* XVII, p.758: Ipso anno (1138) sedicio gravissima inter cives et ipsum episcopum oritur, et vix tandem post magnam tumultuacionem sedatur. For the conflict of 1180, see above, pp.33–4.

Chapter 4

Urban Institutions in the Twelfth Century

It is customary to emphasize the dramatic events of 1106 or of the 1250's, but the independence of Cologne was really won in the peaceful years of the twelfth century. One reason for this peaceful development was that the burghers slowly undermined the archbishop's authority from within. The urban institutions of the twelfth century can be divided into two categories, those directly under the archbishop's authority because they pertained to regalian rights, and those more or less independent of his authority, which arose from the parish communities or the urban community as a whole. It is not by chance that, when this latter group of institutions came to dominate political life in Cologne, the major conflicts between the archbishop and the town erupted.

The first group of institutions were those concerned with administering the regalian rights (justice, the mint, and tolls) that were the core of the archbishop's lordship in Cologne. By the twelfth century, these institutions were to a varying degree under bourgeois control. Most importantly the judicial officials, the minters, and the customs officials were all bourgeois. In addition, the college of *scabini* had expanded its role and had become, in effect, the leading institution of the community. The second group of institutions was only casually related to the archbishop's authority, if at all. In this category belong the parish gilds and later the *Richerzeche* and the town council. These institutions developed from private associations. Although the archbishop attempted to bring them under his control, they did not originally arise from his authority. The second group of institutions played an increasingly important role in urban affairs because they performed indispensable services for the growing town.

Before examining these institutions individually, a word must be said about the general prevalence of community and association in the twelfth century. Various groups and communities were organized, and each group was thought to have its own vested rights.[1] The clearest example is that of the *ministeriales*, who had their rights set down about 1150. The rights of minters, another constituted body, were said to go back to the reign of Rainald of Dassel (1159–67). There are more and more references to the nobles as *nobiles* or *magnati terrae* in the late twelfth- and thirteenth-century charters; they, too, were increasingly considered as an identifiable group. There were also communities with their own rights, such as the peace association and the parish communities in Cologne. In this context, the urban community at Cologne does not appear to be so unusual. Those under the archbishop's authority tended to organize into groups to defend their rights in this period, and the burghers took their place alongside the *ministeriales*, the minters, and the others.

But these constituted bodies were not organized rationally. A clear demarcation among the rights of the various groups did not exist. Nowhere is this more evident than in Cologne itself. The college of *scabini* had an important role in town government, but the bourgeois judges and the parish magistrates also had important functions. Later the *Richerzeche* and the town council developed their own organization and insisted on their own rights. Thus, within the community of Cologne there was not one unified administration, but a group of competing bodies, each with its own jealously guarded privileges. Any attempt to designate one of these bodies as the "sovereign" power within Cologne in the twelfth century the *scabini*, the subjudges, and the parish council in the thirteenth century, and even to some extent thereafter, there were a number of groups and interests each with its own rights, jostling one another for primacy. In general, however, one can say that in the twelfth century the *scabini* the subjudges, and the parish magistrates were predominant, whereas the thirteenth century saw the predominance of the *Richerzeche* and the town council.

A letter of the public authorities of Cologne to Pope Honorius III in 1218 begins with the phrase "*iudices, scabini, universique magistratus Coloniensis.*"[2] These are the three groups most responsible for urban government in the twelfth century. The formulation of 1218 is quite hierarchical and, by that time, rather archaic. The *iudices* (either the

---

1. The idea of freedom or liberties in this period did not involve equality but privilege, not *das gleiche Recht* but *Vorrechte*; cf. Schulz, "Die Ministerialität als Problem," p.219.

2. Lacomblet II 74. The date is approximate.

major judges, the *Burggraf* and the *Stadtvogt*, or more probably their lieutenants) stand closest to the source of legitimate power, the archbishop, and have the widest jurisdiction in the town. The *scabini* are also officials in the archbishop's court although their jurisdiction appears to have been more restricted than that of the judges.[3] The magistrates of the city, that is the parish magistrates, were not directly related to the judicial structure within the *Burgbann* and had jurisdiction only within a given parish. Still, the parish magistrates were in many ways the most important city officials in the twelfth century. The parish communities were stronger than the community embracing all of Cologne, and they were closer to the people. The parish masters sometimes even appear as a group representing the citizens of Cologne. Therefore, the best place to begin a discussion of the communal political authorities in Cologne is with the parish communities and their leaders.

The letter to Honorius III in 1218 is one example of parish magistrates acting as representatives for the entire city. An even clearer example is presented in a document of 1174. Archbishop Philip was preparing an expedition to Italy. To help finance this venture, he received a loan of 1,000 marks from the town, to which he gave in return the proceeds from the mint until the debt was liquidated, and a loan of 600 marks from Gerhard, a customs official, who received the city toll for three years in repayment. To confirm this agreement the archbishop had the clerics, the nobles, and the *ministeriales* of the Cologne diocese swear that in the event of Philip's death they would give no obedience or homage to a new archbishop until he had promised to honor these obligations undertaken by Philip. Those who were called to swear this same oath on the part of the citizens were not the *scabini*, not the judges, not the *meliores* or any similar group, but the magistrates of the parishes. At the end of the witness list they appear again, this time in the company of the *scabini* although the members of neither group are listed individually by name.[4] No other group is presented so clearly in any document of the twelfth century as the representatives of the citizens of Cologne. Still, the magistrates of the

---

3. They had no competence in civil matters in the parishes of Niederich and Airsbach where lower courts with their own benches of *scabini* existed. The judges could and did take part in such civil cases.

4. *Quellen* I 85. In the text: Magistri parrochiarum pro universis civibus similiter firmaverunt. In the witness list: Scabini et magistratus urbis pro universis civibus.

Magistri civium and similar phrases can pose serious problems of interpretation. The parish inhabitant is a *civis*, as is the inhabitant of the

parishes did not form any body with competence in the affairs of the city as a whole. Their activities were normally confined to the individual parishes.

Of the twelve parishes that developed important secular functions, five were attached in some degree to a collegial or monastic church. This group included the four parishes (Severin, Pantaleon, Holy Apostles, Gereon) which formed a ring outside the walls of 1106, but inside those of 1180,[5] and Brigida parish whose parish rights apparently evolved from those of the abbey of St. Martin.[6] Brigida parish was one part of the old market area and, as such, differed little in land use or population from neighboring Martin parish; but the other four parishes attached to collegial churches were in the outlying areas of the town where settlement was sparse and the land was used primarily for agriculture. Another five of these twelve significant parishes developed directly under the authority of the archbishop. These included the four within the old Roman walls (Lawrence, Alban, Columba, Peter) and Martin parish in the market area. Finally, two of the twelve were not parishes at all even though they were called *parochiae* and their inhabitants were called *parochiani*. These were Niederich, lying north of the old Roman walls, and Airsbach, lying south of them. Each included more than one ecclesiastical parish. The centers of the "parishes" of Niederich and Airsbach were lower courts with their own judges and *scabini*.

The development of the parish system in and near Cologne was a long and complex process. There were collegial churches that had parish

---

city as a whole. The *magister civium* may be either a parish magistrate (*Burmeister*) or one of the two urban magistrates (*Bürgermeister*).

Planitz, "Kaufmannsgilde und städtische Eidgenossenschaft," p.73, interprets this document of 1174 to mean that the *Bürgermeister* have won a new role in urban affairs as popular representatives. The *magistratus urbis* in the witness list, however, are the parish magistrates, not the *Bürgermeister*, first because they appear in a parallel capacity to the unambiguous references to the *magistri parrochiarum* in the text of the document, and second because *magistratus* (rather than *magistri*) makes some sense in reference to the numerous parish magistrates but seems strange in reference to only two *Bürgermeister*.

5. Holy Apostles is a partial exception to this since it was partially inside and partially outside the fortifications of 1106.

6. Eduard Hegel, "Die Entstehung des mittelalterlichen Pfarrsystems der Stadt Köln," *Die Kunstdenkmäler im Landesteil Nordrhein* (Köln, 1950), p.82.

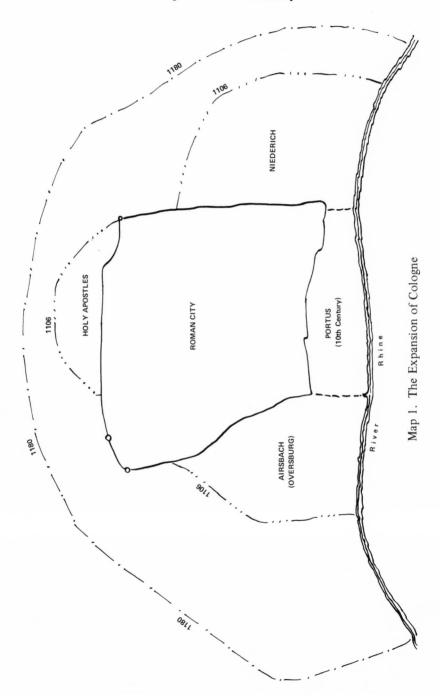

NIEDERICH

HOLY APOSTLES

ROMAN CITY

PORTUS
(10th Century)

AIRSBACH
(OVERSBURG)

River Rhine

1180

1106

1106

1180

1106

1180

Map 1. The Expansion of Cologne

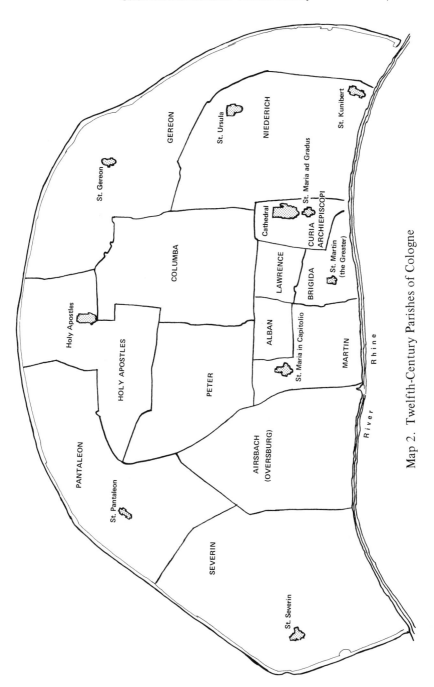

Map 2. Twelfth-Century Parishes of Cologne

responsibilities by the ninth century at least; and they may be even older.[7] But most of the parishes within the Roman walls and in the mercantile quarter were apparently created in the tenth and eleventh centuries.[8] Within the boundaries of these parishes, communities arose. That Niederich and Airsbach were called parishes, even though the local communities arose in conjunction with secular courts there, indicates the fundamental importance of the parish system. Our first sources for parish communities come from the late eleventh and the early twelfth century, and it is probable that the communities arose in the eleventh century. Finally, in the course of the twelfth century, leadership in these communities was assumed by a gild of parish masters. Certain of their activities can be documented in the first town records of the twelfth century. In the course of the twelfth and thirteenth centuries the masters consolidated their position in the parishes until they reached the dominant position reflected in the *Amtleutebücher* of the fourteenth century.

Parish communities with secular functions appear in the first town records, which date from the period 1135–50.[9] In fact, the records we have were drawn up by officials of the parish communities. Foremost among the duties of the parish citizens as neighbors was to witness property transactions. Customarily the witnesses were paid a measure of wine for this service. It cannot be shown that the parish community was active in the ecclesiastical life of the parish at this early date, but it is probable that the parish community was originally attached to the parish church because, later, it still had ecclesiastical duties, such as participation in the synodal court of the parish priest.[10]

---

7. Ibid., p.72, cites a document from 866 which mentions St. Severin, St. Gereon, St. Ursula, and St. Kunibert as collegial churches with parish responsibilities and financial independence.

8. This would obviously be true of Martin parish, which was not settled until after the invasion of 881. Even though the parishes in the old city may have been formed in the ninth century, they did not have control of their own finances and cannot be said to be true parishes at least as late as 891. Cf. Hegel, pp.73–74.

9. In addition to the property records, there is the gild list of St. Martin. (In von Loesch, *Die Kölner Kaufmannsgilde*, where certain men are admitted to the parish community as "geburen." The lists fall into the general period 1135–80.)

10. Thea Buyken and Hermann Conrad, eds., *Die Amtleutebücher der kölnischen Sondergemeinden* (Weimar, 1936), pp.4*–6*.

Parish magistrates also appear in the earliest town records, and there are indications they were already organized in gilds by the middle of the twelfth century. Normally two masters served in each parish for a given period of time, probably a year,[11] but after they left office they were still considered masters. In the Lawrence parish records, which are especially explicit on this point, those identified as masters in any given entry may number from one or two to as many as fourteen or fifteen; furthermore, the same men appear in this capacity over and over again. When one or two appear, the serving masters are meant; when the number varies between eight and fifteen, the whole body of magistrates, including serving masters and past masters, is indicated.[12] That these other parish masters were past masters is indicated by reference to a similar group in Martin parish as *seniores magistri* around 1150.[13]

A parish community and a gild of parish masters existed in the first half of the twelfth century in Lawrence and Martin parishes, but little is known about the internal organization of these parishes. In Niederich, however, a detailed description of the parish community is given in the Niederich *Weistum*. The *Weistum* itself is composed of three parts. The first eight articles describe conditions in Niederich at some time before 1150, probably near the end of the eleventh century;[14] the ninth article describes election procedures current in the parish around 1150. The last five articles of the *Weistum* date from the end of the thirteenth century. Although the *Weistum* gives us valuable information on parish organization, it must be borne in mind that Niederich was atypical because it was based on a secular court and not on an ecclesiastical parish.

---

11. Cf., for example, H. I, p.221 (Laur. 1 VII 8: 1139–52): sub testimonio . . . Dammonis etiam et Herimanni iunioris qui tunc civibus preerant; or H. I, p.18 (Mart. 1 IV 11: 1135–42): coram civibus et magistris civium, tunc vero magisterium tenentibus Tizone, Vollando.

12. The clearest example of this is H. I, p.219 (Laur. 1 V 4: 1135–52): Huius rei testes sunt et erunt omnes magistri civium s. Laurentii, primum illi duo Henricus et Herimannus qui tunc officium deserviebant, insuper et alii quorum nomina hec sunt. . . . Then twelve more parish masters are named.

13. H. I, pp.24–5 (Mart. 2 I 20: 1142–56): Hec facta sunt coram magistris in parrochia s. Martini, Gerhardo et Bertolfo tunc officium tenentibus, et preterea coram senioribus magistris . . . Then thirteen more men are named.

14. Article 8 of the *Weistum* (printed in Konrad Beyerle, "Die Anfänge des Kölner Schreinwesens," *ZRG* 51 (1931), pp.501–3) states: Hec iura

The first eight articles of the document, dating from the late eleventh century, assume the existence of a parish community. The members of the community were privileged and regulated by *traditiones, leges,* and *iura* which had been handed down to them by their forefathers. One joined the parish community simply by acquiring property (*hereditatem aliquam*) in the parish (*inter nos*) and by making the requisite payments to the parish officials. Once this had been done, the parishioners were obligated to help and to defend their fellow citizen against anyone who might make a charge against him.[15] If a parish citizen refused to respond to accusations made against him in parish court, his name was to be struck from the parish list and he was to be expelled from the parish community; furthermore, the parish community would support the accuser in any further legal action taken before the city judges.[16] All cases concerning property held in the parish were to be taken to the parish court and not elsewhere, whether the parish citizen wished to make some legal arrangements concerning his property or whether he had to respond to the accusations of a fellow citizen.[17] Thus by the late eleventh century in Niederich there was a community of landholders which was pledged to help any member as long as he registered his land in the parish court and responded to accusations brought there by any fellow citizen and which could expel any member who failed to live up to his obligations.

Certain parts of the first eight articles of the *Weistum* seem to reflect

---

parrochie nostre antecessoribus nostris tradita sunt ab Arnoldo comite nostro et nobis posteris relicta.

The only Arnold who can be identified as a *Burggraf* or a viscount is the *Burggraf* Arnold who was in office 1082–95. If this is the Arnold meant, it would date the first eight articles in this period. This may be, but it remains questionable.

15. Ibid., (Art. 7). See above, Chapter 3, n.42.

16. Ibid., (Art. 6): Omnis vero civium nostrorum querimoniam facturus de cive suo, coram magistris civium et senatoribus et iudicibus nostris eum interpellet. Si autem ille, qui inpetitur, nequaquam impetenti respondere voluerit et rebellaverit, rebellis de karta civium et communione nostra repudiabitur, et nos impetentem iure suo et sua querimonia ad curiam coram iudicibus adiuvabimus.

17. Ibid., (Art. 2): In his placitis legalibus quilibet civium nostrorum, quicquid de hereditate sua tractare habent vel respondere inpetenti, persolvent et determinabunt apud nos, non alibi, et hoc iure nostro. The plaintiff (impetens) intended here would seem to be a fellow citizen of the parish, as indicated in Article 6 of the *Weistum*. See n.16 above.

the influence of the peace movement. The rebel was to be expelled from the *communio*. *Communio* generally referred to a sworn peace association or a commune in the eleventh century, whereas *communitas* referred to a collectivity of any kind.[18] More than this, the first eight articles end with a curse. Anyone who attempted to break the regulations was to suffer eternal punishment with the devil and his angels.[19] Such ecclesiastical elements in the Niederich *Weistum* recall the peace movement.[20] As we have said, the urban communities of the twelfth century probably did not develop directly from the diocesan peace community of 1083, but some indirect influence is likely. Niederich would seem to be a good example of laymen guaranteeing the peace in place of the ecclesiastically sponsored diocesan organization.[21]

The parish masters, however, seem to have had only a minimal role in the early parish organization. They are mentioned only once, in connection with the accusation of one citizen by another, and then they were to hear the case along with the parish judges and the parish senators. Since the next part of article six of the *Weistum* concerns striking the names of "rebels" from the parish records and since the parish masters were specifically concerned with the maintenance of parish records in the twelfth century, perhaps they are included here for the purposes of witness and registration. In any case, the most important leaders of the parish were the officials of the parish court, the judges and the *scabini* (or senators).

The count and the advocate held three sessions of the court annually at the traditional times (after Christmas, Easter, and Midsummer's Day).

---

18. Vermeesch, p.76; cf. also n.178 where he points out that some confusion of the two terms occurs from the middle of the century.

19. *Das Niedericher Weistum* (Art. 8): Que si quis infidelis et dei adversarius infringere vel adnichilare studuerit, omnipotentis dei odium incurrat et cruciatibus eterne pene cum diabolo et sui angelis in eternum dampnatus deputetur. Amen.

20. Von Winterfeld, "Gottesfrieden," p.36; Vermeesch, p.107, indicates a similar situation at Noyon. Von Winterfeld, pp.42–3, also points out that the seal used by the community of Cologne after 1149 had a picture of St. Peter and the inscription "Sancta Colonia Dei gratia Romane ecclesie fidelis filia." As she indicates, this suggests some indirect influence of the peace movement and some degree of cooperation with the archbishop, who even had the seal used on his documents on occasion.

21. Cf. Vermeesch, p.176: La commune obéirait ainsi à un phénomene général aux XIIe s.: la reprise progressive des institutions de paix par les laiques.

The property transactions and the personal accusations mentioned above took place in the court, and payments of wine or money were made in such cases to the judges or to their vicars, the *ministri*. If the ban was to be laid on the property a further payment of grain to the judge was necessary.[22] It must be presumed, although it cannot be proved, that the judges mentioned here are the city judges, the *Burggraf* and the *Stadtvogt*.[23] The *ministri*, then, would be subjudges in Niederich, analogous to the subjudges in the old city. The decisions of the judges or *ministri* were to be made in accordance with the judgment of the twelve senators of the parish. These senators or *scabini* of the parish are analogous to the *scabini* for the town court, but they were installed by the archbishop or his agent not by the *Burggraf*.[24]

The reference to parish masters in the *Weistum* is the earliest such reference in Cologne. It seems reasonable to assume that the parish masters of Martin parish and Lawrence parish were in office in the late eleventh century as well, since the parish organization in Niederich, like

---

22. *Das Niedericher Weistum* (Art. 1): Comes et advocatus noster tria habent placita legalia: primum post natale domini, secundum post pascha, tertium post nativitatem sancti Johannis baptiste, determinatis diebus. (Art. 3: Si aliquis civium nostrorum domum aut hereditatem aliquam sibi comparaverit presente comite vel advocato, metretam vini ipsis persolvent in ius suum. Si autem ministri nostri, vicarii scilicet eorum, supersunt comparationi supradicte, ipsis denarius I persolvetur in ius suum, et hoc nostro iure tenemus. (Art. 4): Sed si quisquam civium nostrorum insuper bannum ab ipsis iudicibus super hereditatem suam rogaverit, maldrinum avene persolvet.

23. *Comes* and *advocatus* could be used to refer to the *Burggraf* and the *Stadtvogt* respectively, but no sure identification is given in the *Wesitum*. More than this, Article 1 refers to *comes et advocatus noster*, Article 6 refers to *judicibus nostris* and Article 8 mentions *Arnoldo comite nostro*. This insistence on "our count" and "our judges" may indicate that the document means the parish judges. In this case *Arnoldus comes noster* would not be the *Burggraf* in 1082–95 but some parish count who cannot be dated. All of this might be the case, but if so it means there were three sets of judges with interests in Niederich: the *Burggraf* and the *Stadtvogt*, the two parish judges, and the *ministri*, the vicars of the latter. This seems to be too many judges for one parish.

24. Ibid., (Art. 5). The article mentions twelve senators. These can be called either *scabini* or senators. The last section of the *Weistum* (ca.1300) refers to "senatorum scilicet duodecim scabinorum" and again to "scabinus seu senator." In the latter half of the twelfth century the town *scabini* were called both "senators" and "scabini."

the term "parish" itself, was added to a preexistent court community. Furthermore, the development of the parish organization in Niederich in the twelfth century was generally behind that of Martin and Lawrence. Parish records appear later in Niederich and evidence of a gild of past masters is present only by the end of the twelfth century.[25]

The ninth article of the *Weistum* from Niederich is an addition made to the original eight articles around 1150.[26] It describes the method of selecting a parish master or a parish subjudge. The selection was to take place in parish court, and two groups, the parish masters and the parish citizens, had a voice in the selection. If either party refused to consent to the selection, it was invalid.[27] The method of selection probably represents a transition between an earlier stage when the citizens chose their own masters and a later stage, as represented in the *Amtleutebücher* of the fourteenth century, when the gild of masters chose the serving masters.[28] Of course, it is possible that the two electoral groups in the *Weistum* had been established from the beginning of the parish community. In any case, popular participation in the election of masters had been eliminated by the fourteenth century. Whether the *magistri* mentioned are the two serving masters or a gild of past masters is not made clear in the *Weistum*.

The parish magistrates rose to prominence because they performed a service that was in demand, the registration of land transfers and mortgages. Originally whatever registration took place was before the

----

25. Martin and Lawrence are the parishes which provide the earliest evidence for the development of parish activities in most cases. It is difficult to see, however, why Martin should be given precedence over Lawrence. Records begin in both parishes about the same time; the development of the two parishes, as far as we can document it, was parallel. Of course, the gild organization may have been disseminated from Martin parish if we assume that only the merchant gild in Martin could have provided the model for gild development in the parish organizations. Cf. Buyken and Conrad, p.8*, who assume that Martin parish was the first to develop the master's gild.

26. This is indicated by the clause at the end of the eighth article providing for divine retribution against those who attempt to break these regulations and ending with "Amen."

27. *Das Niedericher Weistum* (Art. 9): Si quandoque magister eligendus e[st], quod quidem fiet legali placito, vel si opus fuerit nobis ministro, consensu magistrorum et civium eligantur. Et si alterutra pars horum magistrorum vel civium electioni non consenserint, irrita sit electio.

28. Buyken and Conrad, p.13*.

court and was purely voluntary. It was a convenience for the parties involved, but it added nothing legally to the substantive act of transfer. Nor were the judges or any others in the court responsible for the validity of the transaction on the basis of the document registering the transaction. In the second quarter of the twelfth century in populous parishes such as Martin and Lawrence and somewhat later in the century in other parishes, the parish registry (*Schrein* or *scrinium*) under the control of the parish magistrates became increasingly important. It is from this period that the first actual registrations (*Schreinskarten*) come; however, the judicial functions and the registration functions still had not been separated. In general, the parish magistrates were closely associated with the lower court in their area. This is clear in the Niederich *Weistum*, and is also indicated by the presence of a city subjudge in early transactions in Martin and Lawrence parishes. In the last quarter of the twelfth century the judicial functions were separated from the registration functions, and the officials of a parish acquired a new importance.[29] This was probably accomplished earlier and more completely in parishes where no separate parish court existed. By the thirteenth century it had also been accomplished in Niederich as the second section of the *Weistum* shows.[30]

The earliest entries in the parish registries frequently give detailed information on the registration process that later entries do not provide because the later entries have a more standardized form. For example, around 1140 Heinrich Longus bought the house adjacent to his from a certain Gottfried. The stages of the transaction and the guarantees he sought for it appear quite clearly in the registry entry of Martin parish.[31] First came the formal act, which gave Heinrich substantive title to the property. This act was performed "before the citizens and the parish

29. Ibid., pp.12*–13*.

30. *Das Niedericher Weistum* (section b). The last five articles of the *Weistum*, dating from about 1300, state that the parish judges and the parish *scabini* still preside in the three general parish courts. Otherwise the last five articles are a series of restrictions on the judges and the *scabini*. For example, the *scabini* must be parish residents, and they have no rights in the parish hall except at the three judicial terms. Taken together, the three sections of the *Weistum* (from ca.1090, from ca.1150, and from ca.1300) show that the power of the parish magistrates increased consistently throughout the twelfth and thirteenth centuries.

31. H. I p.19 (Martin 1 V 1): Notum sit omnibus tam futuris quam presentibus, qualiter Heinricus (Longus) emit domum illam domui sue adherentem sibi et uxori sue Elisebedi et eorum amborum liberis pro

magistrates and before the judges (probably the subjudges) and rectors."
Then, to confirm the transaction, he paid the customary fees to the
citizens and to the judges, in order to secure their witness to the fact. This
also involved the registration of the transaction. In this case, specific
reference is made to the registry of the judges *(ad titulum iudicum)* but
obviously it was also registered in the *Schrein* of St. Martin. This served as
proof that the transaction had taken place, and anyone who doubted the
fact of the transaction was specifically instructed to consult the *Schrein* of
the judges where he would discover the truth. As a third step, Heinrich
appeared at the city hall and gave Gottfried's son and heir three marks to
secure further confirmation of the transaction. This last occurred in the
presence of the senators or *scabini* of the town and their "brothers."
Effestucation, as this procedure is known, was also commonly conducted
before the parish magistrates in the late twelfth century. The role of the
senators and the scabinal gild in town affairs, including property cases, will
be discussed later. Of the other two groups involved in this transaction, the
parish magistrates were ultimately the more important. References to the
subjudges as witnesses become less and less frequent towards the end of
the twelfth century. The registry of the judges becomes the registry of the
scabini. And the parish registries controlled by the magistrates' gild achieve
central importance.

By the late twelfth century the individual documents listing transactions (*Schreinskarten*) become more numerous and eventually yield to
more extensive records, documents bound together in books (*Schreinsbücher*). The most important change that took place around 1200,
however, was the guarantee of the validity of the transaction, which the
parish officials assumed on the basis of the registration itself. Before
about 1170 the parish officials were witnesses of the fact of the
transaction and of the fact that no objection had been raised to it. In
the 1170's they began to assume more responsibility in guaranteeing the
substantive validity of the transaction and, especially, in protecting it

---

Godefrido; et hoc fecit coram civibus et civium magistris et coram
iudicibus et rectoribus, et ipse tam firma stabilitate acquisivit, sicuti iure
debuit et sicuti nullius contradictione possidere debet. Ad confirmandum
superscriptum testimonium dedit ipse amam vini civibus, et etiam
iudicibus dedit testimonium, ut sint sibi testes, si opus fuerit, Si aliquis
huic testimonio credere non vult, veniat ad titulum iudicum et videat
qualiter ibi inveniatur veritas confirmata. Post hec quidem idem Heinricus
(Longus) veniens in domum agendarum rerum Godefridi filio et heredi
Ricolfo dedit 3 marc., ut suo consensu hec supradicta confirmata forent,
cuius heredis et sui mundeburdi Sifridi concessu domum illam uxori sue
Elisebedi tradidit presentibus senatoribus et fratribus.

against minor heirs. Thus what had originally been merely a service of witnessing a transaction had become an official function. Such registration still was not obligatory; but it was very convenient, and it developed rapidly.[32]

If we consider the parish communities in the twelfth century, then, certain general conclusions can be drawn. The first basic element of the parish communities was the parish itself or, in the case of Niederich and Airsbach, a court. This provided a territorial element to the community by setting boundaries to the parish unit and including all inhabitants (or at least all landowners) within those boundaries in the parish community, as is indicated in the Niederich *Weistum* from about 1090 and the regulations on St. Pantaleon from 1154.[33] It seems quite clear that the parish organization of Cologne is precisely what it purports to be: the division of Cologne into parishes for ecclesiastical and administrative purposes. Within the confines of these parishes, then, the communities developed. Supposed agricultural communities from the Frankish period or old Germanic hundred courts cannot be found hidden behind the parish system. The only possible exceptions to this might be Niederich and Airsbach, which were parishes in name only and the origin of whose local courts is unknown.

The second basic element of the parish organization was the tasks imposed on the citizens. In the records these involve primarily witness and mutual self-help. The antecedents of these characteristics are unclear. They could have been based on the model of a *Landgemeinde* or that of the merchant gild or that of the peace movement. No direct connection can be shown to any of these, and perhaps it would be best to admit that any or all of these may have had an influence on the development of these characteristics of the parish community. In any case, the merchant gild is not the only possible source of such characteristics and is in a certain respect the least likely source for them since the merchant gild was a voluntary organization while the parish community was a territorial one.

The third basic element of the parish organization was the gild of parish masters. It is important to note that the community was not dependent on the gild for its existence. The gild structure may have been adopted from the merchant gild, and it may have strengthened the burghers in their struggle against the archbishop; but the gild itself was

32. Hans Planitz, "Konstitutivakt und Eintragung in den Kölner Schreinsurkunden des 12. und 13. Jahrhunderts," *Festschrift Alfred Schultze* (Weimar, 1934), p.200.

33. See above Chapter 3, n.27, 42.

superimposed upon or developed out of the parish community.[34] The parish masters appear in the earliest town records, and a special group of past masters is evident in the same records. By the end of the twelfth century the masters have turned their characteristic function of registration into an important element in property transactions. Furthermore, they have virtually supplanted the average citizens and the judges as official witnesses. As the Niederich *Weistum* indicates, they were probably also gaining control of the selection of parish masters.

Little is known about the gild structure or the social organization of the gild in the twelfth century; however, by the fourteenth century the *Amtleutebücher* for the various parishes describe a typical gild structure with serving masters, past masters, and those waiting to become masters. The other elements typical of a gild, selection of the serving masters, selection of those who are waiting to become masters, the annual banquet and the specified gifts, were all set down in detail in the

---

34. This general attitude is expressed also by Buyken and Conrad, p.26*: Während die Sondergemeinden der mehr natürlichen als freiwilligen Zugehörigkeit ihrer Mitglieder zu einem Pfarrbezirk oder zu einer weltlichen Gerichtsgemeinde oder auch der Zusammenfassung in einen hofrechtlichen Verband ihr Leben als Genossenschaften verdanken, sind die Amleutegenossenschaften auf der Grundlage freier Einungen bevorrechtiger Bürger emporgewachsen.

This statement is of particular importance because the authors generally are strong partisans of the "creative bourgeois *Geist*" and the influence of the merchant gild.

In attempting to explain the origins of the parish communities, the major controversy is over the respective roles of the *Landgemeinde* (rural community) and the *Kaufmannsgilde* (merchant gild) in influencing the parish organization. In neither case do the partisans claim that the parish community grew directly from one or the other, but that either one or the other had a preponderant influence on the development within the parishes. This is a part of the more general conflict in interpretation between Steinbach and Planitz.

Ennen, *Frühgeschichte*, p.191–201, gives limited approval to the *Landgemeinde* as a model for parish communities. In Cologne she sees the parish organization of St. Martin as a synthesis of the *Landgemeinde* and the gild and as a model for the other parishes. Ennen, p.201: In St. Martin durchdringen sich Nachbarschaftsgemeinde und Gilde. Aus einer Synthese beider erwächst die Wikverfassung als vorbildliche Organisation für alle Kölner Sondergemeinde.

She does express some reservation on Steinbach's opinion that the principle of mutual self-help was derived from the *Landgemeinde* and not from the *Kaufmannsgilde* (Ennen, pp.195–6).

fourteenth century. Except for the existence of past masters and the probable role of the masters in the selection of new masters, none of the detailed regulations of the fourteenth century can be documented for the twelfth century. But, even if the details of the development are sometimes difficult to identify precisely, the general trend of the development is clear: gradually the gild of parish masters managed to establish their predominance in the parish at the expense of judicial officials and at the expense of the commonalty of the parish.[35]

The model of such a gild organization was, in all probability, the merchant gild of St. Martin. Actually we know very little about the internal organization of the merchant gild in Cologne; however, it probably resembled the merchant gilds for which there is good documentary evidence, such as those of St. Omer and Valenciennes. The organization and regulation of the parish gilds in Cologne in the fourteenth century strongly suggest the organization and regulation of those early merchant gilds.

Probably, then, the gild of masters developed first in the Martin parish. The merchant gild had its seat in the Martin parish, and its distinctive organization surely would have had an impact on parish organization. The merchant gild lists of the twelfth century have been interpreted to show that one was frequently admitted to both the merchant gild and to the parish community of St. Martin at the same time.[36] Furthermore, the masters of the parish gild of St. Martin were almost all members of the merchant gild. This is scarcely surprising in an area as thoroughly mercantile as St. Martin. It is, therefore, all the more significant that the merchant gild and the parish gild were not the same thing. Entrance into one did not automatically mean entrance into the other, nor was it mandatory to be a member of the merchant gild in order to become a parish magistrate.[37] The merchant gild had no direct influence on the institutions of Cologne as a whole, and even in its stronghold of St. Martin, despite its obvious influence, it did not simply become the parish gild. Rather the two gilds existed side by side in the twelfth century, and gradually the parish gild supplanted the merchant gild. It may be that the merchant gild had bequeathed to the parish gild,

---

35. A similar political development is described in John Mundy, *Liberty and Political Power in Toulouse, 1050–1230* (New York, 1954).

36. Von Loesch, *Die Kölner Kaufmannsgilde*, p.3; Buyken and Conrad, p.7*.

37. Steinbach, "Stadtgemeinde und Landgemeinde," p.27; Konrad Beyerle, "Die Entstehung der Stadtgemeinde Köln," *ZRG* 31 (1910), pp.48–9.

and indirectly to other parish organizations, the principles of association and mutual protection. But if this is so, these principles were now embodied in the parish and urban organizations. Consequently, the merchant gild disappears from the records in the twelfth century. It may have continued as a private association, but it ceased to have public significance.

The development of the parish gild of St. Martin in the twelfth century demonstrates both the strengths and the weaknesses of the arguments of those who seek to derive all "progressive" elements in the development of the medieval town of Cologne from the merchants of St. Martin. On the one hand, the typical form of gild organization was probably passed from the merchant gild to the parish gild of St. Martin and thence to the other parish gilds. On the other hand, the notion of community was already in existence in the parishes before the gilds of masters were formed, and, most importantly, the merchant gild was too restricted to become a community, even within the confines of Martin parish itself.

The second group mentioned as leaders of the urban community in the formula of the letter to Honorius III in 1218 were the *scabini*. Whereas the parish magistrates were basically local parish authorities and only occasionally represented more than their own parish, the *scabini* were the body that usually stood for the town as a whole. *Scabini* were assessors at court, who sat with the judge and represented the accumulated knowledge of the customary law. They are mentioned for the first time in Cologne in 1103. That they existed in Cologne—not to mention the important role they played there—sets Cologne apart from the other Rhenish episcopal cities.[38] In 1103 they acted in their typical judicial capacity. The merchants of Liège and Huy complained that the merchants of Cologne had obstructed their rights and forced them to pay duties from which they were exempt. They were especially incensed by the attempt of Cologne authorities to force them to submit to commercial regulations whereby all merchants moving goods across or along the Rhine were supposed to pass through Cologne and pay a duty. Archbishop Frederick restored the rights of the foreign merchants. The decision was made by the judgment of the *scabini* of Cologne.[39] The board of *scabini* was probably older, but we know nothing about them

---

38. Rütimeyer, p.189. *Scabini* were not unusual in more Western cities, of course. Jean Schneider, *La Ville de Metz aux XIIIe et XIVe siècles* (Nancy, 1950), pp.69, 84, points out the similarity between the *scabini* at Cologne and at Metz.

39. *Quellen* I 601.

until the twelfth century. By then almost all of them are clearly bourgeois.

After 1103 the *scabini* are not mentioned again until 1140 when they participated in the archbishop's decision to sell a vineyard.[40] But the interests and activities of the *scabini* did not end with their position on the court. In the second half of the twelfth century, when reference to them becomes more frequent, they are mentioned as senators as often as *scabini*. The new term apparently denotes urban functions beyond a narrow judicial role in the court of the archbishop or *Burggraf*.[41] The senators and their "brothers" (who will be discussed shortly) witnessed the effestucation of a minor heir in the city hall in the case of Heinrich Longus mentioned above.[42] But the clearest early example of the *scabini* or senators as a leading political authority in the new urban community occurs in 1149.

Meeting in the city hall, as urban leaders in distinction to their role as judicial officials in the archbishop's palace, the *scabini* helped to establish a code of regulations for a specialized group of weavers. The document is the first instance of gild regulation by urban authorities in Cologne, and the *scabini* figure prominently in the transaction.[43] It is also the first known use of the city seal; after 1149 the seal appears often. The seal, the symbol of town authority, was in the hands of the *scabini*. In the thirteenth century, when the *scabini* began to lose their predominant position in urban affairs, the seal was guarded by the *Bürgermeister;* but of the two *Bürgermeister,* the one who had to be a *scabinus* controlled the seal. Thus the tradition that linked the city seal with the *scabini* lingered on even after the *scabini* had ceased to be of major importance.[44] The *scabini* also took part in the business of

40. There is no distinction made in the sources between *scabini* and senators. They are called senators in documents dealing with gild regulation (von Loesch I 10: 1149) but in the registry of the *scabini* itself in very similar cases the two words are used interchangeably. Cf. H. II, p.293 (Scab. 1 I 4: ca.1155–65); p.298 (Scab. 1 V 1, 2, 3: ca.1150–80).

41. Lacomblet I 342.

42. H. I, p.19 (Mart. 1 V 1) This is the document concerning Heinrich Longus, mentioned above Chapter 4, n.31. The effestucation took place "in domum agendarum rerum" (the phrase is strange, but presumably the city hall is meant) "presentibus senatoribus et fratribus."

43. Von Loesch I 10. The rights were confirmed . . . in domo civium inter Iudeos sita ab advocato Ricolfo, a comite Hermanno, a senatoribus, a melioribus quoque tocius civitatis vulgi etiam favore applaudente. . . .

44. Heinrich von Loesch, "Die Grundlagen der ältesten Kölner Gemeindeverfassung," *ZRG* 53 (1933), p.149.

registration as indicated above. The registry of the *scabini* did not differ markedly from the registries of the parish magistrates except that their authority covered the whole town and that important families had a greater tendency to use it.[45]

The senators were also representatives of town authority to outside interests. In 1103 the archbishop had guaranteed the rights of the merchants of Liège and Huy by the decision of the *scabini*. In 1171 the merchants of Dinant had their rights confirmed by the senators of Cologne. Certain customs officials (*subthelonearii*) had been infringing on the rights of the copper merchants of Dinant; their actions were repudiated by the higher customs officials (*thelonearii*) and by the senators. The only way the archbishop figures in the case is that Archbishop Frederick, who was dead by then, had granted the merchants of Dinant a charter confirming their rights. This charter was in turn confirmed by the senators.[46] In 1178 a pact was made between the burghers of Verdun and Cologne. It provided that only the merchant who contracted a debt should be held responsible for it and not his fellow merchants from the same town, and it forbade the judicial duel between burghers of the two towns, among other things. The pact was made on the part of Cologne by the counsel of the senators and the "better" men of Cologne (*prudentissimorum*). Here the senators and the "better" men are clearly acting on town authority and as town representatives.[47]

As judicial officials the *scabini* acted alone in cases involving personal dependence and public order. Sometime between 1155 and 1165 a certain Mathilda of Niederich was claimed by the archbishop's chamberlain as a member of the *familia* of St. Peter and, therefore, subject to certain dues that he as chamberlain collected. When she brought the case to court, she was declared free of such burdens by the senator Antonius. The other senators and the people are said to have given their consent to his judgment.[48] It is not completely clear whether the consent of the other senators was merely formal or not, but it is significant that the

---

45. Friedrich Lau, "Das Schöffenkollegium des Hochgerichts zu Köln bis zum Jahre 1396," *Mevissenfestschrift* (Köln, 1895), p.120.

46. *Quellen* I 80.

47. *Quellen* I 90.

48. H. II, p.293 (Scab. 1 I 4): Notum . . . quod Methildis de Nidherich post mortem Gelnoldi viri sui a camerario pulsata et gravata fuit et ad placitum veniens, causa ventilata et secundum iustitiam tractata, a iudicio senatoris Antonii libera ab omni querimonia camerarii iudicata est, consentientibus senatoribus et populo. . . .

decision was made by Antonius alone. This may indicate an increase in the work load for the scabinal court. In minor cases apparently one *scabinus* could make the judgment. By the twelfth century the *scabini* gave the decision in court. The position of the judge in the court, as it was defined in the thirteenth century, was apparently already established in the twelfth century. He presided, but he did not make the judicial decision. His role was limited to delaying the case or, if he wished, arranging a settlement out of court.[49] That Antonius declared Mathilda free from the exactions of the archbishop's chamberlain is also significant. The right of the *scabini* to determine status was clearly of benefit to the emergent town community of free burghers.

Besides competence in questions of personal status, the *scabini* decided cases concerning public order. In three different cases in the latter half of the twelfth century a single *scabinus* condemned individuals "with the consent of the other *scabini*" after accusations were brought. The most colorful concerns a certain Arnold who inflicted three wounds on a pretty woman after a dispute had arisen during a dice game. He was accused in court but did not appear. As a result he was condemned by the senator Gottfried von Stavern and was deprived of all "rights and honor," that is, he was excluded from the community. The conjunction of the judicial role and the communal role of the *scabini* is clearly evident in these cases.[50]

The role of the *scabini* in peace-keeping functions is reminiscent of the Niederich authorities and of the peace movement in general. In the Niederich *Weistum* the parish authorities were empowered to declare as a rebel and to expel from the community anyone who refused to respond to a charge against him. The *scabini* have the same power and the same communal peace-keeping task in these documents from the latter half of the twelfth century. The phrase used to describe the peace they were protecting seems to hark back to the peace movement. The peace is described as a *pax urbana et dominica*; thus there was both a secular and an ecclesiastical aspect to it.[51]

---

49. This is the role ascribed to the judge in articles 7 and 15 of the Great Arbitration of 1258: Lacomblet II 452.

50. H. II, p.298 (Scab. 1 V 1, 2, 3,). These can only be dated generally between 1150 and 1180.

51. H. II, p.298 (Scab. 1 V 2, 3); von Winterfeld, "Gottesfrieden," pp.38–9; see also ibid., p.30, n.70, where she lists the twelfth-century references to phrases such as "universis Christi fidelibus pacem et veritatem amantibus" which may indicate some connection to the earlier peace movement.

The *scabini* did not work alone in urban affairs, but always associated with themselves "good" men of the "better" sort in town (*meliores, potentiores*, etc.). There is no compelling reason to believe that these extra witnesses to a given transaction formed a distinctive body, a "meliorate" as Planitz has called it.[52] But the use of men outside the scabinal college for decisions in urban affairs shows the connection of the *scabini* to the town community and is another indication of the new spirit of town autonomy in the twelfth century. The archbishop did not have a sufficient administration to try to regulate the increasingly complex urban life in Cologne. The relatively peaceful relations between the archbishop and the town in the twelfth century demonstrate that, if he did not appoint the *scabini* as administrators of the town, at least he did not object to their exercise of power. In the thirteenth century, when violent conflict between the archbishop and the town was the rule rather than the exception, he objected to new town leaders who had arisen in the intervening period precisely because they were not bound to him by oath as lord of the town, in the way the *scabini* were. In short, the government of the town was principally in the hands of the *scabini*, and one probable explanation for the relative peace in Cologne in the twelfth century is that they were felt to be in the service of the archbishop.

The *scabini*, like the parish masters, were organized in a gild structure, and the evidence for the existence of the gild comes from roughly the same period (1135–50) for both groups. Unlike the parish masters, however, it is those waiting to be chosen as masters (the so-called *fratres scabinorum*) who appear first and most frequently in the documents rather than the serving master of the gild or the past masters. The *fratres scabinorum* appear in the records for the first time in the period 1135–42.[53] In 1178 twenty-two brothers of the *scabini* are mentioned, and they appear frequently in documents in the latter half of the twelfth century. The brothers of the *scabini*, as well as the *scabini* and the parish masters, were given the task of resolving future disputes in the agreement of 1178 with Verdun.[54] One serving master

---

52. Planitz, "Kaufmannsgilde und städtische Eidgenossenschaft," pp.69–76, elaborates a "meliorate" thesis, which will be considered in more detail later. He lists most of the relevant sources for other groups associated with the *scabini* in town affairs.

53. The oft-mentioned Martin 1 V 1 (H. I, p.19).

54. *Quellen* I 90 (1178): Si vero debitor pecuniam quam mutuo accepit sicut iustum est reddere remuerit ipse creditor si debitorem testimonio

of the scabinal gild, Gerhard the *thelonearius*, is mentioned in 1171,[55] but for the rest evidence of a gild structure is lacking in the twelfth century. There can be no doubt that a gild structure existed, but precisely how it was constituted and what its regulations were are not known for this early period.

At least by 1235 the *scabini* had control over the election of serving *scabini* and the *fratres scabinorum*.[56] As in the parish gilds of officials, the dominant influence in the scabinal gild in the thirteenth and fourteenth centuries was the past masters. Not all members of the fraternity could necessarily serve as *scabini* in a judicial sense. Installation by the *Burggraf* and an oath to the archbishop were necessary for that. But it is probable that most of the past masters were also judicial *scabini*. The typical payments of wine, wax, and cakes made by the master of the gild to the gild members in the fourteenth century were also made to the *Burggraf* and the *Stadtvogt*, who were still theoretically the judicial superiors of the *scabini*.[57]

The *scabini* were the only group that served consistently as an authority for the urban community in the twelfth century. Solidified by associational ties, they played a predominant role in urban affairs well into the thirteenth century.

The *iudices* mentioned in the formula of the letter to Honorius III were less important than the *scabini*. In a sense they occupied a more exalted position than the *scabini* because they were the representatives of the *Burggraf* and the *Stadtvogt*, but they can only be shown to have performed significant urban functions in the period 1100–1160, after which the *scabini* and other town authorities gradually supplanted them. Whether by choice or by persuasion, the major judges, the *Burggraf* and the *Stadtvogt*, were increasingly excluded from urban affairs. They appointed the subjudges (called *comes, vicecomes, subcomes*, or *greve* in the one case and *advocatus, secundus advocatus, subadvocatus* in the other) but they always appointed burghers. Koebner has attempted to present the subjudges as concessions achieved by the *conjuratio* of 1112,

---

duorum virorum qui Scabini sint vel confratres Scabinorum vel officiales colonie convincere potuerit bona sua ei restituantur. . . .

Further references to the *fratres scabinorum: Quellen* I 74 (1159); H. I, p.164, n.1 (1182); H. II, p.293 (Scab. 1 I 2: 1150–61).

55. *Quellen* I 80: Gererdus thelonearius magister senatorum.

56. Lau, *Schöffenkollegium*, pp.129–30.

57. Ibid., p.110.

but his attempt has not been successful.[58] It is more probable that the expansion of urban justice in commercial matters, land transactions, and questions of public order simply did not interest the major judges, one of whom was a noble and one of whom was a landed *ministerialis*. They naturally wanted to maintain their rights and incomes, but they were also anxious to delegate their authority. This desire was a common one, and can even be seen among the customs officials, who delegated some of their duties to *subthelonearii*.

The major judges could still be active in Cologne affairs on occasion. In 1159 the acquisition of land in Marsdorf by St. Gereon, mentioned above, was accomplished "by the judges in the presence of the senators and the citizens." The judges mentioned in the witness list are Heinrich the *Burggraf*, Hermann the *Stadtvogt*, Albero the viscount (*subcomes*), and Hermann the subadvocate (*subadvocatus*).[59] As late as 1237 the *Burggraf* allowed himself to be persuaded (by a financial consideration) not to exercise his right to tear down structures on public property. And in 1231 he intervened in a case in Niederich concerning public ways and building regulations.[60] But in most cases the subjudges represented the major judges, and the latter were absent. In the gild regulation of 1149 and in a number of property cases up until the last few decades of the twelfth century, it is the subjudges who appear, not the major judges. Property cases could be transacted at the general courts held three times a year; but even here the parish magistrates were active, and registry entries in which the subjudges are not mentioned are common early in the twelfth century.

The first references to subjudges come from the beginning of the twelfth century (certainly in 1106, perhaps in 1103)[61] but they do not appear in documents very often after 1160, and by 1180 they are gradually pushed into the background by the *Bürgermeister*. The personal and financial relationship between the major judges and the

---

58. Koebner, pp.297–306. His argument, which strains the evidence, has been refuted by Luise von Winterfeld, "Neue Untersuchungen," pp.13–4.

59. Lacomblet I 74.

60. Lacomblet II 220. *Quellen* II 124. See above, Chapter 2, n.34.

61. *Quellen* I 601 (1103): Hermannus advocatus, Ludochinus advocatus. The first is the *Stadtvogt*; the second may be a subadvocate.

Lacomblet I 269 (1106): Franco comes et Wolframmus secundus comes. Almerus advocatus et Rutolphus secundus advocatus.

subjudges in the early period is not known; however, in 1198 *Burggraf* Heinrich of Arsberg pledged the *Burggrafschaft* to Simon de Macellis for a loan of 200 marks. Simon received in pledge a house and land, which the *Burggraf* owned in the city, and the whole jurisdiction of the *Burggrafschaft* except the three general courts *(wizzehliche dinge)* and the control of public lands *(ruminge* or *Räumungsrecht)*.[62] The sum of 200 marks is considerable, and it must be presumed that the *Burggraf* had substantial income in the town besides the rights he reserved to himself. Some of these sources of income have been mentioned before, such as the traditional gifts of the gild of *scabini*, rights over the Jews, and rights in the mint. Presumably the pledge also involved other judicial income such as the jurisdiction concerning land transfer according to Cologne law, which involved traditional payments of grain and wine. Simon was to retain the pledge for at least four years, after which the *Burggraf* could redeem it. Simon was the viscount in this period, and his identification with the office was so strong that he retained the title *comes* after he was no longer in office.

These three groups, the parish magistrates, the *scabini*, and the subjudges, were the most important leaders in Cologne in the twelfth century. Of the three, two were intimately concerned with one of the regalian rights, justice. The third, the parish magistrates, owed their chief importance to authority separate from that of the lordship of the archbishop. Other groups concerned with regalian rights were of importance in the twelfth century, specifically the customs officials and the minters. They, like the *scabini* and the subjudges, were persons of bourgeois background who helped to administer rights and income of the archbishop that had clearly devolved from higher authority.

The archbishop's chamberlain was responsible for the archbishop's income from the tolls; however, the task of collecting the tolls was delegated to customs officials or *thelonearii*. In the twelfth century they were all prominent burghers. In some, perhaps in most, cases the *thelonearii* did not personally collect the tolls but delegated their authority to *subthelonearii*. Until 1152 the toll was entrusted to a *ministerialis*. Werner, the first known member of the important Jude family, is indicated in Cologne sources before 1150 as both a *ministerialis* and a *thelonearius*.[63] It is likely that the toll was granted as a ministerial fief. There was danger, however, that such a grant might become hereditary, and in 1152 the king ruled that the *Tafelgüter*, or

---

62. H. II, pp.302–3 (Scab. 2 III 5).

63. Lacomblet I 300 (1125): *Wernherus tunc coloniensis thelonearius* is listed under the *ministeriales*.

that income pertaining to the *mensa* of the cathedral, including the toll, could not be granted in fief or otherwise alienated.[64] After 1152 the toll was farmed or used as repayment for a loan as in the cases of the *thelonearii* Gerhard Ungemaz in 1174 and Constantine of St. Lawrence around 1180.[65]

The designation *thelonearius*, like that of *comes*, tended to attach itself to a man even when he was no longer active in the office. *Thelonearii* figure prominently in town documents from the middle to the end of the twelfth century, so prominently that one historian of Cologne institutions wants to see in them all-important town leaders, the original *Bürgermeister*, around whom the gild known as the *Richerzeche* arose.[66] This position is hardly tenable, but the *thelonearii* were important men individually. They never formed a gild, perhaps because the archbishop kept better control over them than he did over the minters and the *scabini*. The availability of the income from tolls as a security for loans may well have been the most important consideration for the archbishop, a consideration that would be less obvious in the case of judicial revenue or the mint. In any case, the *thelonearii* are important as individuals, not as a group, and in the thirteenth century the designation itself disappears.

The minters, the other group closely associated with one of the regalian rights, did form an important gild, but little is known about them individually; as far as we know they did not play a significant role

---

64. Lacomblet I 375: Post hec vero in eadem urbe memoratus domnus Cunradus tercius romanorum rex in celebri curia a multis ac precipuis regni principibus iudicium requisivit super bonis a mensa seu elemosina coloniensis archiepiscopi alienatis et idem principes et tota regio curia iudicium dedit quod cottidiana servicia ad episcopalem mensam pertinentia nequaquam inbeneficiari vel invadiari iure possint eo quod regno et ecclesie debeantur . . . et omnia bona que prefatus Arnoldus II. venerabilis coloniensis archiepiscopus his fretus iudiciis recollegit scilicet teloneum urbis colonie et multa episcopalia servicia nemo ab ipsius usu et potestate suorumque successorum avellere presumat.

65. *Quellen* I 85 (1174); H. II, p.300 (Scab. 2 I 4: ca.1180–84).

66. Hoeniger, "Die älteste Urkunde," pp.280–1. The position taken by Hoeniger is untenable. It is based primarily on the fact that *thelonearii* appear at the head of urban witness lists in the mid-twelfth century and the subjudges begin to appear less frequently at the same time. Then after 1180 the *thelonearii* are scarcely mentioned, and the *Bürgermeister* begin to appear in official capacities. This much is true and significant for the role of the *thelonearii* in urban affairs in the twelfth century; but no connection can be shown between the *thelonearii* and the *Bürgermeister*.

in the urban community as a group until the thirteenth century. In the frequent disputes over the minters' rights in the thirteenth century, Archbishop Rainald of Dassel (1159—67) is mentioned as the one who granted the minters their rights. The minters may originally have been functionaries personally dependent on the archbishop and members of his *familia*. The usual designation for them was *Münzerhausgenossen*, and *Hausgenossen* would seem to refer to an origin among the personal dependents of the archbishop. Perhaps Rainald of Dassel organized them into a separate body and discontinued their dependent status. Certainly the minters of the late twelfth and thirteenth century were wealthy and privileged men, and most of them, if not all, were probably bourgeois. The entrance fee into the minters' gild is not known for Cologne; but in Worms a new minter had to pay two gold pennies and one-half ounce of gold to gild the bishop's staff; in Strassburg the fee was half a gold mark, five gold pennies, and one pound of silver pennies; and in Mainz it was two lots (or one ounce) of gold.[67] Obviously minters had to be wealthy men. Two masters of the mint are mentioned in the parish lists of St. Martin in the twelfth century, and one of these was a member of the merchant gild.[68] For the most part, however, information on individual minters does not exist.

The customs officials and the minters, like the *scabini*, were officials responsible to the archbishop; but ultimately the most important institutional developments took place in groups only very indirectly responsible to the archbishop, if at all. The parish gilds, which fall into this category, have already been discussed. The most important innovation of the urban community was the town council or *Rat*. It appeared very late in Cologne, making its first tentative appearance in 1226. Its development belongs more properly to the thirteenth century. The other significant institution that developed independently of the archbishop's authority was the *Richerzeche*.

The word *Richerzeche*, or in its more usual form in documents *Richerzecheit*, means the eating and drinking club of the rich and powerful.[69] Thus the name itself emphasizes the social aspects and the

67. Rütimeyer, p.81.

68. Ibid., p.77: Anselm and Marcmann. Another minter appears in the list: Heremann *monetarius*. Cf. von Loesch, *Die Kölner Kaufmannsgilde*, p.55. Heremann was also a member of the merchant gild. Others related to money matters are included in the lists, such as Otto *examinator argenti*.

69. Friedrich Philippi, "Die Kölner Richerzeche," *Mitteilungen des Instituts für österreichische Geschichtsforschung* 23 (1911), p.89.

gild form of the association. The *Richerzeche* was of special importance because its masters were the *magistri civium* or *Bürgermeister* for the whole city. In contrast to the serving masters in the parish gilds, the *Bürgermeister*, that is the serving masters of the *Richerzeche* gild organization, were able to maintain their relative power against the past masters, of course, but the *Bürgermeister* had duties of their own above public authority with a competence comparable to that of the *scabini* in the twelfth century or that of the town council in the thirteenth century. The only public task it performed as a body was the regulation of craft gilds. It indirectly performed a public service in electing its masters, of course, but the *Bürgermeister* had duties of their own above and beyond those of their gild. They held a kind of police court for insult or injury by word or deed and served as urban officials in other capacities.[70] The gild as a whole had no rights in these matters. Eventually the *Bürgermeister* even became more dependent on the town council than on the *Richerzeche*.

The first sure reference to the *Richerzeche* comes from the period 1179–82. In that period the officials of the *Richerzeche* issued a charter confirming the rights of the turners in the town hall.[71] Thus, by about 1180, the officials of the *Richerzeche* were regulating gilds, their distinctive function. The officials of the *Richerzeche* were half *scabini* and half non-*scabini* because one of the serving masters had to be a *scabinus*. The only document concerning gild regulation before 1180 is the one mentioned before which regulated a specialized group of weavers in 1149. It was issued in the city hall by the subjudges, the senators, and some of the better men of the town (*meliores*) and with the common consent of the town as a whole. The *Richerzeche* is not mentioned.[72] Thus the *Richerzeche* achieved a public role in gild regulation sometime between 1149 and 1180. Certainly the *Richerzeche* arose before 1180. The large number of officials or past masters mentioned in the document of 1180 would place the origin back several years.

Whether the private gild developed around public officials, the *Bürgermeister*, or whether the leaders of the private gild later became public officials cannot be ascertained. All attempts to find the *Bürgermeister* in sources before 1180 have failed. Perhaps, one could

---

70. The additional duties of the *Bürgermeister* are indicated in the Great Arbitration of 1258: Lacomblet II 452, articles 26 and 37 (p.246).

71. Von Loesch I 13. The document was drawn up ". . . in domo burgensium in capitulo officialium de richirzegcheide."

72. Ibid., 10.

hazard a guess that the *Richerzeche* did indeed originate before 1149 as a private gild led by two masters, that, in other words, the private gild antedates the public duties. The relatively independent position of the serving masters of the gild against the position of the past masters would be an argument against such a conjecture, but the list of past masters in 1180 seems to suggest a long prior history for the gild. What can be stated with certainty is that the *Richerzeche* did not enjoy its one public function until after 1149.[73]

Politically the *Richerzeche* was an alliance of the families represented among the *scabini* and certain other prominent families not represented among them. That one *Bürgermeister* had to be a *scabinus* and that he was the one who guarded the city seal indicates the importance of the *scabini* in the *Richerzeche*. In this sense there is a certain parallel between the document of 1149 and that of 1179–82. The *scabini*, originally a judicial group meeting at the archbishop's court in his palace, associated others with themselves when they undertook urban tasks in the city hall. The document of 1149 depicts a decision in an urban court of *scabini* and subjudges, supported by some other worthy people from the community and, almost as an afterthought, with popular acclamation. This appears to be a judicially based urban assembly. Although *meliores* should not be given a technical meaning, it is still significant that the *scabini* and the subjudges felt obligated to include other important men in their decisions in urban affairs. Even the populace at large is mentioned, probably indicating here for the city at large a development from popular participation to gild control in urban affairs parallel to that in the election of parish magistrates. The *scabini* and the subjudges required popular support. In 1149 they received it from the better sort and the common sort of citizens. By 1180, at least, certain of the *scabini* had joined some of the "better sort" in a private

---

73. Planitz, "Kaufmannsgilde und städtische Eidgenossenschaft," pp.29 and 69ff., and von Winterfeld, "Neue Untersuchungen," p.18, among others, attempt to show that the *Richerzeche* arose from the *conjuratio* of 1112. The weakness of the reference has already been indicated. That the *Richerzeche* did not appear publicly until ca.1180 poses an additional obstacle to Planitz and the others. They insist that the *Richerzeche* was present covertly in the twelfth century, even in the gild regulations document of 1149 where the *meliores* stand for the *Richerzeche*. The supposed reason the *Richerzeche* does not appear before 1180 and only in a subordinate position thereafter is the archbishop's reluctance to give it recognition. Planitz, pp.72–5, is forced into unbelievable contortions to prove his point.

gild that regulated the rights of craft gilds. It is also significant that the subjudges have disappeared in the document of 1180. For the ever growing enterprise of city government, the competence of the subjudges and the *scabini*, in the narrow sense of their duties, was too restricted. The positions of the subjudges and of the *scabini* were filled with burghers, but that was not enough. They had to involve other members of the town community. In this process the subjudges lost their old significance as representatives of authority from above, and the *scabini* were transformed from a judicial body to a group with responsibilities in leading the community of Cologne. The lordship principle was slowly and gradually replaced with the communal principle. It is not sufficient, probably not even possible, to go back to 1106 or 1112 for the foundation of the commune. More significant is the gradual evolution of institutions in the relative peace of the twelfth century.

In this process the development of the *Richerzeche* is of cardinal importance, despite the gild's limited competence. It represents a transition from the first form of development, the capturing and strengthening of the old lordship institutions by the bourgeoisie, to the second form, the emergence of new insitutions which were private in the sense that they were independent of the authority of the lord. This independence was precisely what angered the archbishops of the thirteenth century. They were especially concerned about the *Richer-zeche* for this reason. But by that time it was too late to reverse the development that had already taken place, as the arbitrators of the conflict between the town and Archbishop Conrad of Hochstaden pointed out in 1258: the *Richerzeche* had a fixed place in the customary procedures of the town.[74] The *Richerzeche* was also private in another sense. In a development analogous to that in the parishes, the common citizen was excluded from the communal task of gild regulation. "Medieval urban democracy" can be a greatly inflated term; it did not exist in its ancient or modern sense in medieval Cologne. But there was a tendency to exclude the commonalty altogether from town government and to invest authority instead in private gilds and privileged bodies, which were restrictive and had overlapping membership. In short, a patriciate emerged and the participation of the common citizen in political life was more restricted than it had been before.

---

74. Lacomblet II 452. See below, Chapter 6, n.3.

Chapter 5

The Patriciate, 1074–1230

Distinctive urban institutions arose and flourished in Cologne in the twelfth and thirteenth centuries. These were the means by which urban affairs were organized, and eventually they were the instruments by which the autonomy of the town was established. But who developed these institutions? Who profited by them, worked through them, gained prestige from them? Who were the political leaders in Cologne from the first dramatic episode of resistance in 1074 until the victory of the town over the archbishop in the thirteenth century?

In this investigation the customary term *patriciate* will be used only in the narrow sense of a political elite. Records which demonstrate political activity, especially office holding, are abundant. Most evidence for economic activity or social status, on the other hand, is much more fragmentary and subject to varying interpretations. Where it is possible, the social and economic evidence that helps to define the patriciate will be presented and compared; but, in order to give some definition to an amorphous term like *patriciate*, it will be considered primarily a political elite.

No one is entirely satisfied with the term *patriciate*. It is neither contemporary nor precise. But it belongs to that class of terms, which, if they did not exist, would have to be invented because, at the very least, it alludes to a phenomenon whose existence is not challenged.[1]

---

1. Friedrich von Klocke, *Das Patriziatsproblem und die Werler Erbsälzer* (Münster, 1965), p.16, indicates that the term patrician was used in 1306 for the patriciate in Brussels; however, as he points out, the term was not generally used until the fifteenth and sixteenth centuries. He attributes this change in usage to humanistic education.

Erich Maschke, "Continuité sociale et histoire urbaine médiévale," *AESC* 15 (1960), pp.936–48, offers two definitions of "patriciate." First,

The first town records in Cologne distinguish between the "greater" and the "lesser" citizens, between the "better sort" and the common people. Thus, already in the twelfth century as far back as our records go, a distinction existed between a *patriciate* and the rest of the town's inhabitants.[2] It is usual to regard a patriciate as a virtually closed caste enjoying legally defined rights of predominance and leadership. This is not true of most medieval towns, certainly not of Cologne. In Cologne, the elite was not closed to new men, nor was it a ruling group defined in law. This makes the group much harder to define. But, elusive and imprecise as it is, a distinction between the greater and lesser citizens does exist in the records. Not founded in law, it was firmly based on prestige and on deference, in a society where social distinctions were taken for granted.

---

a patriciate may mean a group of rich and powerful families, intermarried, which constituted the higher social ranks of the town, even though their special position lacked juridical sanction. Second, a patriciate may mean a group who held a monopoly on municipal offices before the craft gild revolts of the late fourteenth century. Obviously, the latter definition is the more useful one.

Much the same definition is provided by Philippe Dollinger, "Patriciat noble et patriciat bourgeois à Strasbourg au XIVe siècle," *Revue d'Alsace* 90 (1950–51), p.52, n.1. He introduces various other qualifications which are of little importance for Cologne in the twelfth and thirteenth centuries, but basically he defines the patriciate as a group of families (*lignages* or *Geschlechter*) who by their landed and mobile wealth dominate their city into the fourteenth century and especially those who have access to the town council.

Schneider, *La Ville de Metz*, pp.114 and 128, finds that the *paraiges* that made up the patriciate in Metz had originally been family groups. Further he believes that landed wealth and a connection to the *familia* of the bishop or of other churches in Metz were more important originally than mobile wealth or mercantile activity. In Metz these *paraiges* dominated political life more completely than in many cities.

This emphasis on families and on political officeholding is the one used in this study because it is the most workable definition.

2. Twelfth-century examples of this are given below. Franz Steinbach, "Zur Sozialgeschichte," p.175, indicates that a distinction between the *cives primores* and the *cives minoris ordinis* existed in the eleventh century and was probably much older. Lambert of Hersfeld, "Annales," *MGH. SS.* V, pp.211ff., in discussing the revolt of 1074, refers frequently to the *primores* of the city, meaning the leaders of the opposition to the archbishop.

Medieval writers did not use the word *patriciate*, or any variation of it, to designate the urban elite; however, thirteenth-century sources do refer to *geslechte* (*Geschlechter*) or, in Latin, *genera*. The family, in the sense of the *Geschlecht* or the *lignage*, is basic to any definition of the patriciate.[3] It was common for certain families to supply office-holders over the course of a century, or even over the course of several centuries. In fact, by the thirteenth century most urban governing bodies filled vacancies through co-optation, and it was usually a son or a nephew who was co-opted.[4] Whatever else a patriciate may mean, then, it is primarily—in the terms of the age itself—a collection of families.

Wealth was also a prerequisite for membership in the patriciate. If a citizen were not independently wealthy, he could not afford to devote some of his time to public affairs; and others would not acknowledge his leadership without this indispensable qualification. The Parfuse family rose to wealth and prominence in the twelfth century, but failed financially in the thirteenth century and, as a result, lost their political influence. They attempted a futile comeback in the fourteenth century, but their financial failure necessarily entailed their political failure. They still appear in town records, but now they are "lesser" citizens, not patricians.[5]

Without wealth no one could be a patrician, but wealth itself did not guarantee the status of a patrician, if this is defined in political terms. There were wealthy families in Cologne who did not hold office. The Quattermart family held extensive property in Cologne in the twelfth century. They continued to prosper but only began to hold office in the fourteenth century.[6] Of course, it is always possible that they wielded

---

3. Steinbach, "Zur Sozialgeschichte," p.181. *Genus* is used in the sense of *Geschlecht* in town documents of 1252 and 1263; *geslechte* is used by Gottfried Hagen in *Dit is dat boich van der stede Colne*, which was written about 1270 and which describes the patrician wars of the thirteenth century.

4. A clear example of co-optation among the *scabini* is provided by a record of the selection of *scabini* from ca.1235–37 given by Friedrich Lau, "Das Schöffenkollegium des Hochgerichts zu Köln bis zum Jahre 1396," *Mevissenfestschrift*, pp.129–30. Eight new *scabini* were chosen. Five of them were sons of the fifteen *officiales scabinorum* who made the selections; the other three came from the powerful Overstolz and von der Ehrenpforte families.

5. See below, pp.112–3, for the Parfuse.

6. A genealogy and references for the Quattermart family are given by Freidrich Lau, "Das Kölner Patriziat bis zum Jahre 1325," *Mitteilungen* 26

political influence behind the scenes or that politics simply did not interest them. Even if these suppositions could be substantiated, which they cannot, there are enough families whose members do not attain office until the second or third generation to suggest that wealth was a basis for mobility into the patriciate but not sufficient by itself.

The twelfth-century sources provide ample evidence of the distinction between the more powerful citizens and the weaker citizens in Cologne, but no evidence that the more powerful citizens formed a legally defined, closed group with its own privileges. In 1171 the archbishop of Cologne established regulations for the *scabini* at Andernach. He stated that fourteen *scabini* were to be chosen for life from among the wisest, best, and most powerful men (*ex prudentioribus . . . melioribus . . . potentioribus . . .*); this restored the status of the *scabini* and ended the scandalous state of affairs in which they had been chosen "not from among the best and richest and most powerful men . . . but from among the poorest and most humble."[7] Clearly if the *scabini* of Andernach had

---

(1895), pp.135–36. Luise von Winterfeld, *Handel, Kapital, und Patriziat in Köln bis 1400* (Lübeck, 1925), pp.21–2, discusses the Quattermart family. They will not be discussed in detail here because their rise to political prominence came only in the fourteenth century.

In the early twelfth century the abbey of St. Pantaleon accepted a man whom the patricians denounced as a *plebeius nummatus*. Thus from the beginning there were rich men who were not considered patricians. It is interesting that "plebeian" is used here although its counterpart "patrician" is not. Steinbach, "Zur Sozialgeschichte," p.183; von Winterfeld, *Handel, Kapital, und Patriziat*, p.5.

Von Klocke, *Das Patriziatsproblem*, pp.9–21, has introduced the term *Honoratiorenschaft*, or a group of rich men who were not members of the patriciate, into the discussion of medieval urban social groups. The Quattermart indicate that there were rich men outside the patriciate in twelfth-century Cologne, if the patriciate is defined politically; but evidence of a group, even loosely defined, of *honoratiores* is lacking. The term *honoratiores* is used in Cologne in the twelfth century, but as von Klocke himself points out (p.16) it is equivalent there to *meliores* and thus refers to the patriciate, not to an *Honoratiorenschaft*.

7. Heinrich Beyer, Leopold Eltester, and Adam Goerz, eds., *Urkundenbuch zur Geschichte der jetzt die Preussischen Regierungsbezirke Coblenz und Trier bildenden mittelrheinischen Territorien* II (Coblenz, 1865), no.5 (1171). The document states that the regulations are modeled after those in effect for the *scabini* at Cologne. It is interesting that the *scabini* at Andernach also have the right of co-optation in filling their vacancies and that it is foreseen that they may be away from Andernach for commercial reasons.

to have these qualifications, then the *scabini* of Cologne had to have them too. A similar attitude is expressed in the settlement the abbot of St. Martin and a group of bourgeois laymen reached over the administration of a hospital in Martin parish. One provision of the agreement was that,

"if any lay brother is stricken by age or illness and wants to enter the hospital, he shall receive permission. For there shall be private rooms set up in such a way that such men may remain in them quietly and without being a burden to the others and, according to what they are able to provide, he who has been more honored and mightier in the world shall be treated more honorably and with more care . . ."[8]

There are numerous references to "those citizens who are more important by age and by authority," to the illustrious, better, or more powerful men. In the records of the town itself in the twelfth century, some men are entitled *dominus*.[9] But, for the most part, the words used indicate a predisposition to think in terms of rank and power rather than in terms of well-defined groups. The very variety of the terms themselves leads to this conclusion.

Some medieval towns apparently had well-defined patriciates. In Ghent the *viri hereditarii* were families who held land in full property (*hereditates*). They took steps to ensure that this property remained in the same circle of families, held a special right of gracious jurisdiction, and were the circle from which the urban *scabini* were chosen.[10] No definition of this kind can be found in Cologne. *Hereditates* were held by many families in Cologne. Quite probably the Cologne patricians had to hold *hereditates*, but the number of families that held them is too large to equate it with the patriciate. The group of people who witnessed charters, sometimes called the *viri probabiles*, was a more restricted group, but its members always performed their function in

8. *Quellen* I 58 (1144–47): Si quis fratrum laicorum senio vel egritudine confectus hospitale ingredi voluerit, non ei negetur. Sint etiam private camere seorsum huiusmodi deputate, ubi quiete et sine offensione ceterorum tales maneant et ubi secundum hoc quod facultas suppetit et expedit qui fuit honoratior et mollior in seculo, honoratius et accuratius tractetur. . . .

9. There are many examples that could be cited; references to some of the most important are given by Planitz, "Kaufmannsgilde und städtische Eidgenossenschaft," p.70, n.3.

10. Hans van Werveke, *Gand: Esquisse d'histoire sociale* (Brussels, 1946), p.31–2.

conjunction with the *scabini* or at the behest of some important figure. Again, the rights and privileges of the patricians at Cologne were fewer and less well defined than those of the patricians at Ghent.

In 1182 the abbot of St. Martin closed a charter by saying, "we have taken care to have this charter signed by others along with us and to affix our seal to it; the names of the witnesses by whose wise (*prudenti*) counsel and with whose reliable (*probali*) witness we have confirmed this transaction are these: . . ." Then comes the witness list including dependents of the abbey, some *scabini*, brothers of the *scabini*, *burgenses*, and many other *viri probabiles*.[11] *Prudens*, referring to wise counsel, occurs in other documents in twelfth-century Cologne. Strictly it should apply, as here, to the actual counsel and deliberation, but the *viri prudentissimi* are also equated with the *viri probabiles* because those whose advice was sought were also used as witnesses. The *viri probabiles* had to be men of substance, men whose word would be believed; furthermore, they had to be men of a status high enough that they could witness or testify in any eventual legal transaction that might arise from the original transaction. In short, they had to be worthy or credible witnesses (*probabiles*). Not surprisingly, the point at which the sources are most explicit is on the matter of worthy witnesses.

The craft gild document of 1149, the first document from Cologne which was drawn up in the city hall and to which the city seal was appended, indicates that a group of the better men of the town (*meliores totius civitatis*) participated along with the judges and *scabini*. The second step in this transaction was a confirmation "no less valid than the first and no less necessary for the gild, namely the witness of men who are illustrious and the most trustworthy of all the citizens."[12] As I have indicated elsewhere, this group of *meliores* is not the *Richerzeche*; but it is significant that the judges and *scabini* usually involved a group of prominent men in official transactions. For our purposes, the *scabini* and the *meliores* together represent the political

---

11. H. I, p.164, n.1: . . . hanc cartam conscribi et nostri sigilli inpressione signari curavimus, subscriptis testibus quorum prudenti consilio et probali testimonio istem traditionem confiravus [sic] quorum nomina hec sunt. . . .

12. Von Loesch I 10. The document was issued . . . in domo civium inter Iudeos sita ab advocato Ricolfo, a comite Hermanno, a senatoribus, a melioribus quoque tocius civitatis vulgi etiam favore applaudente. . . . Sequitur et alia confirmatio priore non minus valida nec fraternitati minus necessaria testimonium videlicet virorum illustrium et tocius civitatis probatissimorum, quorum nomina subsequuntur assignata. . . .

elite or the patriciate in twelfth-century Cologne. Near the end of the twelfth century (ca.1180) when the *Richerzeche* was formed, the two groups were organized in institutional form, but the basis had been laid before, probably as far back as the troubles of 1106.[13]

For our purposes, then, the patriciate was a political elite which can be identified in the documents as office-holders (*scabini*, officials of the *Richerzeche*) or as witnesses (*meliores*). It was composed of families who frequently maintained political power in their own ranks through several generations and who had considerable wealth in land, rents, and, presumably, commerical enterprise. It was a group which was ill defined, a group to which entry was always open through wealth or a timely marriage, but also a group which tried increasingly to restrict the benefits of political power to itself.

Not all of the men prominent in political affairs in the twelfth century founded patrician families, and some families pass out of the town records very quickly. Some of the great families of the thirteenth and fourteenth centuries were already established in the twelfth century, but many do not appear until the thirteenth century. In the following section the individual families will be considered in the following order: first, those men or families prominent in the twelfth century that for one reason or another did not pass their influence in town affairs on to their descendants; second, those families that arose in the twelfth century and were a part of the patriciate in the thirteenth and fourteenth centuries; and third, those families that rose to prominence in the period 1190 to 1230 and that were part of the later patriciate. In all cases four basic questions will be posed: first, what offices were held by members of the family; second, what significant property and other forms of income did members of the family possess; third, what was the origin of the family; and fourth, how long did the family remain in power. All of these questions cannot be answered for each of the

---

13. It seems to me that this much of Planitz's theory on the "meliorate" is valid. Cf. Planitz, "Kaufmannsgilde und städtische Eidgenossenschaft," p.69–76. The judges and *scabini* did involve other particians in the business of government; *meliores* is one of the characteristic designations given to this group of patricians who did not hold offices. I cannot agree, however, with Planitz's contention that the *Richerzeche*, as the authority of the merchant-led commune, really represented the town even though the archbishop at first refused to recognize it, then recognized it tacitly, and then even considered its functions illegal as late as 1258. It is contortions such as these (Planitz, "Kaufmannsgilde und städtische Eidgenossenschaft," p.72) that make the hypothesis unworkable.

families, but the evidence is a sufficient basis for some conclusions and speculations on the nature of the patriciate in Cologne, and these will follow the individual family sketches.

A number of important political figures in the twelfth century did not establish patrician *Geschlechter*. The most outstanding example is Gerhard Ungemaz (Immoderatus). Either Gerhard or his father of the same name appears as a parish official in the earliest records of Lawrence parish.[14] Lawrence was an unusual parish. Within its bounds were the precinct of the cathedral and the archbishop's palace and the Jewish quarter as well. The city hall was also located there, so that Lawrence represented the political center of the town, as Martin and Brigida represented the commercial center. The magistrate lists of Lawrence parish, wherever they allow us to know something of the magistrates who witnessed property transactions, demonstrate the unusual characteristics of the parish. The same lists that include Gerhard Ungemaz contain the names of at least three converted Jews and, in one entry, the name of the archbishop's butler.[15] Gerhard Ungemaz the Younger lived in a house across from the archbishop's palace, in an area that included city properties belonging to the greater *ministeriales* of the archbishop, such as the Schilling and the von Alpheim families, who had their chief seats in the countryside; their only urban property was in this area. It is presumably from the location of this house that Gerhard is sometimes called *de curia* rather than from any close connection to the archbishop's court.[16] Gerhard the *thelonearius* appears in one list as

---

14. H. I, p.218 (Laur. 1 IV 4: ca.1135–52) Gerhard is found frequently in other parish magistrate lists of the period; and, even though his "name" Ungemaz is not given, his position in the list is sufficient to indicate that Gerhard Ungemaz in meant. Characteristically he is listed together with his kinsman (*cognatus*) Hartwich Harde. The lists include many men with their sons, their brothers, or their kinsmen. Since Gerhard Ungemaz the *thelonearius* did not die until the 1190's, it may be that this Gerhard is his father. In fact, the first loan made by Gerhard the *thelonearius* in the period 1159–70 (H. I, p.237: Laur. 3 II 10) is made by "dominus Gerardus *Iuvenis* de curia."

15. H. I, pp.217–22, passim. Thiderich and Eckebret with his son Fordolf are each identified as "Judeus." In an early entry (Laur. 1 IV 2) Eckebret is described as one "qui Judeus fuit." "Giselbertus pincerna archiepiscopi" is listed among the magistrates in Laur. 1 VI 1 (ca.1135–52).

16. When the convent of Weiher described Gerhard's property left to them by his step-daughter Richmud, his house was described as "domum

a *ministerialis*. In 1182 he witnessed a document along with the holders of the high ministerial offices, and he is also listed among the *homines* of the abbey of St. Martin in 1190.[17] But usually he heads the list of the *burgenses* or *cives* in distinction to the *ministeriales*. Marriage also provides a hint of the connection of the Ungemaz family to the *ministeriales*; Gerhard's sister Hadewig was married to the butler Winemar.[18]

Despite the fact that he is once listed among the *ministeriales*, Gerhard Ungemaz is distinguished primarily in urban affairs—first, as a *thelonearius* and a *scabinus* and second, as a moneylender. He was a *thelonearius* by at least 1171 when he and Karl of the Salzgasse, as the *magistri thelonearii*, were called upon to restrain the unjust practices of their *subthelonearii* against the rights and privileges of the merchants of Dinant.[19] In the witness list of this document Gerhard is also identified as the *magister senatorum*, a designation which otherwise is lacking in Cologne documents of the twelfth century. Throughout the 1170's and 1180's Gerhard appears as a *thelonearius* and as a *scabinus*.[20] In the document of 1179–82 he appears as an official of the *Richerzeche*.[21]

In addition to his residence Gerhard had a number of properties in the parishes of Lawrence, Niederich, Martin, and Columba. He acquired these in most cases either through purchase or through the default of a debt owed to him. In fact, Gerhard appears to have been one of the most important moneylenders in Cologne in the latter half of the twelfth century. Sometime in the 1160's he lent the *Stadtvogt* the rather minor sums of 25m. 5s. and, on another occasion, 8m. (the latter in conjunction with another man) as well as 16m. to the sons of Richwin Canus.[22] After 1170 the records left of Gerhard's moneylending indicate larger sums. In the 1170's (perhaps in 1174) he received a house from Archbishop Philip as a pledge on a loan of 50m., which the archbishop needed for an Italian expedition. Philip had to repay the

---

ex opposito palacii archiepiscopi, quam ipse inhabitare solebat, que vendita fuit duci Brabancie pro 300 marcis 25 marcis minus," the last apparently referring to a sale made by Weiher.

17. Lacomblet I 481; *Quellen* I 105.

18. On the *pincerna* Winemar, cf. H. I, p.278, n.2.

19. Lacomblet I 441.

20. Hoeniger, "Die älteste Urkunde," pp.259–60, provides a list of these citations.

21. Von Loesch I 13.

22. H. I, p.235 (Laur. 3 I 22), p.236 (Laur. 3 II 5, 10).

loan within six weeks of his return to Cologne or else the house was Gerhard's. It was further stipulated that no archbishop other than Philip could redeem the pledge. Apparently the house passed to Gerhard.[23] In 1178–79 Gerhard lent 40m. to Ludwig, the examiner of the mint; in 1191–93 120m. to a certain Heinrich.[24] But the largest loan Gerhard made, of which we have a record, is the 600m. he lent to Archbishop Philip during the preparation for an Italian expedition in 1174.[25] In return for this large sum Gerhard was to receive the toll of the city for more than two years, to dispose of as he would. The document incidentally provides the information that Gerhard had been farming the toll, for he gives the archbishop 600m. "beyond that which is now owed or will be owed (from the toll)."[26]

In addition to his well-documented activities as *thelonearius, scabinus,* and moneylender, Gerhard was probably the subadvocate of the city around the years 1166–67 and certainly an advocate of the monastery at Valindrin.[27] Gerhard Ungemaz de curia died in 1197 or 1198 about the same time as his nephew Gerhard.[28] But, typical for twelfth-century Cologne, Gerhard's family played an important role in town affairs, too.

Gerhard's brother Dietrich was the subadvocate of Cologne and is usually designated as *advocatus in curia.*[29] Gerhard, the son of Dietrich

---

23. H. I, p.251 (Laur. 4 III 6). Entry 4 III 13 shows Gerhard and his wife in possession of the house "quam domnus archiepiscopus Philippus in sua propria possessione habuerat."

24. H. I, p.130 (Mart. 8 VII 5), p.208 (Mart. 14 I 24).

25. Lacomblet I 452.

26. Ibid.: Gerardus quoque ante curiam sexcentas marcas nobis prestitit super universi reditus solutionem, que nunc nobis debetur et postea debebitur. Ipsi theloneum ciuitatis usque ad proximum pascha disposuimus, annis quoque duobus sequentibus in potestate sua dedimus, cui uel quomodo concedi debeat.

27. Lacomblet I 418; Lacomblet IV 631. It would be interesting to know if there were any connection between the sums Gerhard advanced to the major advocate (*Stadtvogt*) of Cologne and the position of subadvocate he held under him; however, no evidence exists for such a connection. On Valindrin: H. I, p.339 (Col. 1 VI 14, 20): ... et domnum Gerardum thelonearium quem sibi ecclesia advocatum elegerat. ... The significance of *dominus* in reference to Gerhard or other burghers, here as elsewhere, seems to be only a title of respect. .

28. H. I, p.278, n.4.

29. Cf., for example, H. I, p.277 (Laur. 5 VIII 7).

and the nephew of Gerhard the *thelonearius*, is also called *de curia*. The designation probably indicates that they, too, lived in that area of Lawrence parish where Gerhard the *thelonearius* had his residence. Dietrich appears as the *secundus advocatus* in a document of 1178 regulating trade between Cologne and Ghent.[30] Otherwise he and his son do not appear in the records in any official capacity. Apparently they were never *scabini*, members of the *Richerzeche*, or the like.

Much of the information about this family has come down to us because they founded a convent. About 1197 or 1198 both Gerhard the *thelonearius* and Gerhard, the son of Dietrich the advocate, died. A certain Richmud was left as the widow of the younger Gerhard; she was also the step-daughter of Gerhard the *thelonearius* since he had married her mother.[31] Richmud inherited most of the property of her step-father and her husband and, after the other heirs had renounced their rights in it, used it to establish the convent of St. Mary of the Pond (*Weiher* or *piscina*). Most of the property consisted of houses in Cologne, but it also included four and a half *mansi* of agricultural land and five *iurnales* of vineyard which her husband had had planted in an area near the town.[32] The tradition of the convent called Gerhard the *thelonearius* "a knight who was famous throughout Germany" and called her husband Gerhard a knight as well. It is doubtful that Gerhard the *thelonearius* was that well known, but the designation *miles* may well be accurate. An entry in the registry of Lawrence parish shortly after 1200 refers to Gerhard the former husband of Richmud as a *miles*.[33] Thus the later and doubtful tradition of the convent is supported by roughly contemporary evidence.

There can be little doubt that this was one of the richest and most prestigious families in Cologne in the late twelfth century; however, in the thirteenth century the family all but disappears. The only line that can be followed into the thirteenth century is the line of Dietrich the

---

30. *Quellen* I 91. He is listed among the burghers after his brother Gerhard *thelonearius* and before the viscount Vogelo. All of them are listed before the *scabini*. Winemar the butler, and the brother-in-law of Gerhard and Dietrich, is also included in the witness list, after the *scabini*.

31. H. I, p.278, n.3.

32. H. I, p.285, n.1.

33. H. I, p.286, n.2. In this context *miles* seems to be a general social designation, "knight" as opposed to "soldier" or "vassal." As such, it would be parallel to the tendency in thirteenth-century documents to refer to the *ministeriales* of the archbishop as *milites*.

subadvocate. He had three sons and a daughter: Gerhard, already mentioned, Heinrich, Johann, and Hadewig. Of these, only Heinrich had descendants of whom we have knowledge. None of them was of any importance in town affairs. Whether they lost their position and their wealth or whether they simply turned to other pursuits is not known. The only interesting bit of information we have on these thirteenth-century relatives of Gerhard the *thelonearius* is a connection to the monastery at Rees. Johann, the son of Dietrich the subadvocate, was a cleric at Rees and his nephew Rainald was the *scholasticus* there.[34] But no one from the family was important in the political affairs of Cologne after 1200.

The Minnevuz are another family whose political influence is apparent only in the twelfth century. The most important member of the family, Hermann Minnevuz, was a viscount of the city in the 1140's and 1150's and a *scabinus*. His son Heinrich was a *frater scabinorum* and a *scabinus* and his brother Conrad and his grandson Gozwin were *scabini* in the latter half of the twelfth century and the beginning of the thirteenth century.[35] None of them seems to have been a member of the *Richerzeche*. After the reference to Gozwin as a *scabinus* in 1218, they disappear from political life in Cologne. Gozwin is included among the *ministeriales* of the archbishop in 1211.[36] There is no evidence that any of the other Minnevuz were *ministeriales*. Gozwin's grandfather, Hermann the viscount, always appears among the *burgenses* or the *senatores* in the witness lists.[37]

Rainer of Basel and Bertrad were the parents of Hermann Minne-

---

34. Lau, appendix to his patrician genealogies in the *Kölner Stadtarchiv, Karte* 21.

35. Hermann as *comes*: H. I, p.72 (Mart. 4 IV 15), p.36 (Mart. 2 IV 2, 3), p.26 (Mart. 2 I 32); as *scabinus*: Heinrich Schäfer, ed., "Inventare und Regesten aus den Kölner Pfarrarchiven," *Annalen* 83 (1907), p.4. Heinrich and Conrad as *scabini*: ibid., p.165. Gozwin as *scabinus*: *Quellen* II 59.

36. Richard Knipping, ed., "Ungedruckte Urkunden der Erzbischöfe von Köln aus dem 12. und 13. Jahrhundert," *Annalen* 74 (1902), p.192. By comparing this reference to the one in 1218 for Gozwin as *scabinus*, it is clear that one could be both a *scabinus* and a *ministerialis* at the same time.

37. *Quellen* I 59; Schäfer, p.4. Wilhelm Pötter, *Die Ministerialität der Erzbischöfe von Köln vom Ende des 11. bis zum Ausgang des 13. Jahrhunderts* (Düsseldorf, 1967), lists Hermann Minnevuz as a *ministerialis* in 1147 on the basis of Lacomblet I 246; a better version of the same document (*Quellen* I 59) places Hermann among the *burgenses*.

vuz.[38] The most important piece of property held by Hermann and his descendants was a house and some stalls in the quarter of the cloth merchants near the city mint. Apparently Hermann inherited this property from his mother.[39] The house in which both Hermann and Heinrich lived was in the butchers' quarter of Martin parish. It may well have been part of the dowry received by Hermann from his wife.[40] Hermann also owned a house in the old market, and his son Heinrich owned one in the saddlemakers' quarter.[41] All of these properties were in the mercantile parish of St. Martin. No positive identification of the Minnevuz as a mercantile family exists, but it must appear likely from their property holdings and their descent from Rainer of Basel.

In the thirteenth century the family disappears from Cologne records. Gozwin, the last of the Minnevuz to appear in these records, became a *ministerialis* and a knight. Whether he died while still a burgher, or whether he established himself somewhere outside the city, is not known.

Gerhard Ungemaz is mentioned as a *ministerialis* and as a *homo sancti Martini* and Gozwin Minnevuz became a *ministerialis*, but we cannot be certain in either case that they were descendants of *ministerialis* families of long standing. In at least one well-documented case, however, a *ministerialis*—and an imperial *ministerialis* at that—did become a burgher.

Richolf, who is variously described as *iudex*, *scultetus*, or *villicus Aquensis*, apparently came from the family of the mayors of Aachen although no evidence remains that he ever exercised that function himself. It is certain, however, that he was a *ministerialis* of the

38. H. I, p.26 (Mart. 2 I 32). It is possible to imagine, then, that the family was originally Swabian and probably mercantile. The sister of Bertrad was married to Hermann Stolzegrano, who is mentioned in the gild list of St. Martin and who had some connection, perhaps commercial, with an abbey in Bavaria. (*Quellen* I, p.149: *Bürgerverzeichnisse*; H. I, p.23: Mart. 2 I 13. Also cf. von Winterfeld, *Handel, Kapital, und Patriziat*, p.8). If this is so, then Gozwin was a burgher who became a *ministerialis*.

39. H. I, p.26 (Mart. 2 I 32). The entry makes it clear that it is Hermann's mother's sister (*matertera*) and her husband who renounce their claim in one half of the property.

40. H. I, p.72 (Mart. 4 IV 15). Hermann receives the income for life " . . . in dimidia domus illius parte in platea Reni site, que fuit uxoris sue Mathildis; post mortem suam eadem pars ad liberos Mathildis hereditet. . . ."

41. H. I, p.67 (Mart. 4 II 2), pp.94—5 (Mart. 6 II 10, III 6).

emperor. He witnessed a charter of Frederick Barbarossa in this capacity in 1174 and is clearly shown acting on the emperor's behalf in a document of 1179.[42] Sometime in the 1170's he apparently moved to Cologne. He is listed under the rubric *ministeriales* in the witness list of an archiepiscopal document of 1176 along with the *Stadtvogt*, the chamberlain, and the marshal.[43] It would be possible to imagine that Richolf was transferred as a *ministerialis* from dependence on the emperor to dependence on the archbishop of Cologne. Such cases were not uncommon in the twelfth century. But the document of 1176 is the only reference which indicates that Richolf may have been a *ministerialis* of the archbishop. However he may have passed from the ranks of the imperial *ministeriales*, he became after 1176 a *scabinus* and eventually a member of the *Richerzeche*.[44] In the 1170's Richolf held land and houses in the parishes of Columba, Martin, and Gereon.[45] According to an entry in the registry of the *scabini* between about 1167 and 1172, his uncle Karl the *thelonearius* had sold him some land described as "*predium in silva et campis et areis*," but the location of the land is not indicated.[46] Richolf of Aachen is the clearest example of a *ministerialis* who passed into the ranks of the leaders. But his career is undoubtedly atypical, and it is probably significant that he appears increasingly in the documents as a *scabinus* or even a *burgensis* and not as a *ministerialis*. Town leaders of the twelfth century were recruited

---

42. Hoeniger, "Die älteste Urkunde," p.258, who cites Butkens, ed., *Trophées du duché de Brabant* (The Hague, 1724) I: *Preuves*, p.43.

Lacomblet I 470. The abbot of Burscheid had acquired some land at Vilen, which he had certain *fideles* of the emperor receive since the abbey lay under the jurisdiction (*ditione*) of the emperor. Four such *fideles* are mentioned, including *Ricolfum iudicem Aquensem*. It is probable that the document was issued some years after the fact, at a time when Richolf's interests were already primarily in Cologne.

Pötter, p.24, misses this aspect of Richolf's life completely.

43. Lacomblet I 459.

44. He is listed as a *scabinus* in 1176 (Lacomblet I 455) 1178 (ibid., 464) and 1180 (ibid., 474). He is listed as an official of the *Richerzeche* in the document of 1179–82 (von Loesch I 13) and, interestingly enough, is listed under the *burgenses* in distinction to the *ministeriales* in a charter of 1185 (Lacomblet I 501).

45. Hoeniger, "Die älteste Urkunde," p.258, provides information on his property. The property in Gereon was probably extensive; it is described as a "curia cum domo" (H. II, p.220: Ger. 1 IV 31).

46. H. II, p.295 (Scab. 1 III 4).

from several social groups, but to be effective they had to become burghers. Richolf was not a leader imposed from outside, but a burgher, who only chanced to differ from his colleagues in background.

Some of Richolf's influence can be attributed, perhaps, to family connection. His mother's brother Karl held a number of positions in Cologne from 1150 to his death in 1183 or 1184. He appears among the *optimates civitatis* as a witness for the abbot of St. Martin as early as 1152. By 1159, at least, he was a *thelonearius* and by 1171 a *scabinus*.[47] There is no hint that he may have held the rank of *ministerialis* until a document of 1183 in which Karolus de Salzgassen and his son Karolus are listed as *ministeriales s. Petri*, i.e., *ministeriales* of the cathedral.[48] Karl held land and houses in the mercantile parishes of Brigida and Martin as well as that country land that he sold to his nephew and an urban estate, the Covoltzhof, which he received in hereditary tenure from the *Burggraf* Heinrich von Arsberg.[49] Karl was dead by ca.1183−84 because the registry of the *scabini* indicates that his daughter Durechin asserted her rights to Covoltzhof at that time.[50] Whether any other children survived Karl is not known; in any case, any possible descendants of Karl, or of Richolf, cannot be followed after the 1180's. They did not form the basis for a patrician *Geschlecht*.

A fourth family prominent in the twelfth century was the de Hoie family. They came presumably from the town of Huy in the Liègois.[51] The first member of the family to be mentioned in Cologne records, Markmann Hoier (Hoger, de Hoie) appears as a witness in the period 1140−59. Various categories (*burgensium honoratiores, viri illustres*) under which he was placed in this period indicate his importance; by 1154, at least, he was a senator. He was also a past master of the Martin

---

47. *Quellen* I 65. Karl is listed as a *thelonearius* before the *scabini* in witness lists of 1159 (Lacomblet I 399) 1176 (ibid., 461) and 1178 (*Quellen* I 91). He is listed among the *scabini* in 1171 (Lacomblet I 441) 1176 (ibid., 455) 1178 (ibid.,464) and 1180 (ibid., 474). He is described as Richolf's *avunculus* in the entry of the scabinal registry concerning the sale of land already mentioned. (H. II, p.295: Scab. 1 III 4).

48. Lacomblet I 490.

49. Hoeniger, "Die älteste Urkunde," p.264; for the Covoltzhof: H. II, p.295 (Scab. 1 III 6).

50. H. II, p.296 (Scab. 1 III 7).

51. Hoeniger, "Die älteste Urkunde," pp.265−6, provides a genealogy and the pertinent references. He omits mention of the children of Markmann Hoier, who did not in any case have a political career.

parish organization.[52] Markmann's known property was in Martin parish. He held valuable property among the cloth merchants, in the Rheingasse, and in the market.[53] Although there is no conclusive evidence, it is not difficult to imagine Markmann Hoier as the son of parents who came to Cologne from Huy as merchants, settled in the mercantile quarter of St. Martin, and carried on the family business— possibly in the important cloth trade. It is significant here that Emelrich, the son of Markmann's brother Emelrich, is included in the gild list of St. Martin.[54] Little is known about Markmann's children except their names (Ulrich, Pilgrim, and Guda) and that they did not personally do business in the shop in the market they inherited from their father. Indeed, it cannot be demonstrated whether Markmann ever worked there.[55]

Still, Markmann Hoier was not the only prominent member of his family. Either his brother or his nephew Emelrich is listed among the

---

52. As a senator in 1154 (Schäfer, p.4) 1155 (L. Korth, "Urkunden aus dem Stadtarchiv von Köln," *Annalen* 41 (1884), p.102) and 1159 (*Quellen* I 74); as a *senior magister* of Martin parish sometime between 1142 and 1156 (H. I, pp.24–5: Mart. 2 I 20). He was a witness to several important affairs, including the first extant document establishing craft gild regulations in Cologne in 1149 (von Loesch I 10).

53. H. I, p.68 (Mart. 4 II 10): hereditas inter venditores pannorum. Its value is shown by the seventy marks that Markmann's son Ulrich was able to raise, using one third of the property as security: H. I, p.80 (Mart. 3 I 6).

H. I, p.105 (Mart. 7 I 16): domus iuxta Renum.

H. I, p.84 (Mart. 5 II 14, 15): a *taberna* and a *cellarium* in the market area. A *taberna* was apparently a shop rather than a stall since the *cellarium* or storage area is described as *situm sub taberna*.

54. *Quellen* I, pp.153–4: *Bürgerverzeichnisse*. The identification is not certain, but *Emelricus filius Methildis*, who is mentioned twice in the lists is probably Emelrich de Hoie.

55. The possession of this distinctively mercantile property indicates the problems of generalization from the sources at our disposal. The *taberna* and the *cellarium* were apparently the property of Markmann Hoier since his children as a group grant the *taberna* to Emund and the *cellarium* to Johann for four years. Perhaps Markmann actually used the shop for his business, if indeed he was a merchant (no firm evidence exists even for this latter point although the circumstantial evidence seems to indicate it). In any case, Markmann's sons, Ulrich and Pilgrim, did not use it, for they granted it to Emund, who is described as actually using it (*in qua stat Emundus*). Did Markmann's sons have another base for their

viri illustres of the city in 1149, and another nephew Markmann Lämmchen became a senator or *scabinus*.[56] The son of Markmann Lämmchen, Markmann Wievelruz, appears as a member of the *Richerzeche* in the first extant document of that institution.[57] Both Markmann Lämmchen and Markmann Wievelruz were sometimes called *de suburbio* (or de Oversburg). Presumably, then, their residence was in Oversburg (i.e., Airsbach) although the only sure records we have indicate property in Martin and Niederich.[58] After Markmann Wievelruz the family cannot be followed.

Finally, as an example of the diversity in the origins of the twelfth-century patriciate, the de sancto Laurentio family, Jewish in origin, should be mentioned. The first identifiable members of the family are Eckebret Judeus (*qui Judeus fuit*) and his son Fordolf, who

---

father's presumed business? Did they give it up altogether and turn to other pursuits? There is no answer to be found in the sources. It is important to indicate, in any case, that possession of mercantile property does not necessarily mean a mercantile occupation—as is evident in the case of the sons of Markmann Hoier.

56. Emelrich frater Marcmanni witnessed the gild regulation of 1149 (von Loesch I 10). Whether the elder or younger Emelrich is meant is not clear. Hoeniger, "Die älteste Urkunde," p.266, calls the younger Emelrich a *Schöffensenator* but he presents no evidence for this designation. Markmann Lämmchen (Lembechin, Agnellus, or de suburbio) appears as a witness between 1140 and 1178 (references in Hoeniger, "Die älteste Urkunde," pp.265–6). He is indicated as a senator in 1155 (Korth, "Urkunden aus dem Stadtarchiv," p.102) 1169 (Beyer, et al., eds., *Urkundenbuch . . . mittelrheinischen Territorien* I 658) and 1178 (*Quellen* I 90, 91).

57. Von Loesch I 13. Hoeniger, "Die älteste Urkunde," p.265, lists references to him as a witness between 1166 and 1200. He also identifies him as a *scabinus*, but this rests only on a probable forgery (Lacomblet I 434, the document concerning the *Stadtvogt*).

58. Hoeniger, "Die älteste Urkunde," p.265; Lacomblet I 474. Property records: Hoeniger, "Die älteste Urkunde," p.265 (Mart. 4 II 27, 28; 5 II 9; 7 I 21; 17 I 3). Hans Planitz and Thea Buyken, eds., *Die Kölner Schreinsbücher des 13. und 14. Jahrhunderts* (Weimar, 1937), no.535. H. II, p.72 (Nied. 2 III 7).

59. H. I, p.218 (Laur. 1 IV 2, 4: ca.1135–52) and several other entries in the Lawrence parish records. Fordolf's son Helperic was also a magistrate in Lawrence parish: H. I, p.241 (Laur. 3 IV 6: ca.1159–72). Von Winterfeld, *Handel, Kapital, und Patriziat*, pp. 13–14, discusses the family.

were magistrates of Lawrence parish in the mid-twelfth century.[59] Fordolf's son Constantine held the toll at Cologne from the archbishop in the 1180's for an annual payment of 350m. until the debts the archbishop owed him were paid.[60] Constantine was probably married twice; the division of his inheritance among the five children of his second marriage indicates that his wealth was in real as well as mobile property. Nine and a half houses, a tower, and some workshops were left to his children.[61] Aside from the parish magistrates already mentioned, apparently the only member of the family who held an office was Constantine's son of the same name, who is mentioned as a *scabinus* in 1237.[62]

These five families represent the diversity of those prominent twelfth-century families that did not continue as powerful families in the thirteenth century. Although precise information is difficult to find, they seem to have varied origins. Richolf of Aachen was definitely a *ministerialis*; the ancestors of the Minnevuz and the de Hoie families were probably merchants who immigrated to Cologne from other cities. The de s. Laurentio family, the least important of the five families, was Jewish in origin. The properties held show few significant differences. Typically a twelfth-century patrician held market land, some properties in the old city or the other parishes, and some rural land, usually in the fields near Cologne. Another typical feature is the use of a larger piece of property as a suitable residence for a town notable, such as the Covoltzhof held by Karl the *thelonearius* from Heinrich von Arsberg. The offices held typically included the *scabini* or senators and, in this period, the *thelonearii*. By the end of the century, many of the same men or their heirs compose the *Richerzeche*. Thus a bourgeois pattern of life—perhaps even a patrician pattern of life—can be established for many twelfth-century leaders; but the question of origins and even the question of occupation remain open.

There are many other individuals who can be identified as office-holders in the twelfth century, but who did not form patrician

60. H. II, p.300 (Scab. 2 I 4: ca.1180–84): . . . et tam diu obtinebit Constantinus teloneum donec omne quod tenetur ei reddere dominus archiepiscopus recipiat debitum.

61. Constantine married to Friderun: H. I, p.253 (Laur. 4 IV 17). They had a son Helperic and a daughter Engilrad: H. I, p.249 (Laur. 4 II 11); H. II, p.317 (Scab. 2 XII 9); Planitz and Buyken, *Schreinsbücher*, no.723. Constantine married to Elizabeth: *Quellen* II 156 (1234–5); Constantine is dead as the inheritance is divided.

62. *Quellen* II 166.

Geschlechter. In fact, the greater number of such office-holders in the twelfth century in comparison to the thriteenth century suggests that the patriciate was not very closed in the twelfth century and tends to support Lestocquoy, who states that the urban patriciates only began to establish themselves fully in the period 1170 to 1200.[63] Evidence for the other twelfth-century office-holders is more fragmentary than for a family like the Ungemaz, but some of it is useful in helping to establish a pattern for the twelfth-century leaders.

Emund de Macellis is a clear example of a merchant who was a *scabinus* in the twelfth century. He is mentioned as a *scabinus* or senator in the period 1155–80 and was an official of the *Richerzeche.*[64] He held property principally in Martin parish although he also acquired some in the Jewish quarter of Lawrence parish. In the 1160's he acquired a shop (*taberna*) in the market among the cloth merchants from the children of Markmann Hoier for a period of four years. This was the shop in which he already transacted his business.[65] Various individuals, some of them important like the viscount Simon and his brother Richolf, are called *de sub macello* or *sub macellis* in the early thirteenth century, but no connection to Emund can be shown, nor is it necessary to imagine one. The name does not appear to be the name of a *Geschlecht.*

Wolbero, *filius Sigewini,* is another example of a leader who was probably a merchant. He is mentioned as a *scabinus* in 1178 and 1180.[66] His father was Sigewin the viscount, who is mentioned frequently in charters of the mid-twelfth century.[67] Sigewin was a parish master of Martin parish and is listed in the merchant gild lists of

---

63. Lestocquoy, "Fils de riches," p.148.

64. References in Hoeniger, "Die älteste Urkunde," p.257.

65. H. I, p.84 (Mart. 4 II 14). The significant phrase is: taberna in qua stat Emundus. The Emund in this entry is identified only as being married to Gertrude, but it is probable that Emund de Macellis is meant since the name is uncommon in the twelfth century and since his wife's name was Gertrude. Hoeniger, "Die älteste Urkunde," pp.257–8, uses the rarity of Emund's name to suggest that he is probably the same Emund who in 1142 appears in a witness list behind his brother Hermannus filius Razonis. If this is so, and it must remain doubtful, then Emund would be part of the important Raitze *Geschlecht*.

66. *Quellen* I 90, 94.

67. Lau, *Beamten* p.70. In office: ca.1126–36, frequent references after that until his death in 1159.

Martin parish as is his son Wolbero.[68] He was also selected by the monastery at Hirsau as an advocate for some of its property located in Cologne. His own property was located in Martin parish, in the market area and in the Rheingasse.[69] He died in 1152, and his funeral services were at St. Gereon.[70]

Evergeld Suevus appears as a *frater scabinorum* in 1178 and as a *scabinus* in 1180.[71] The designation "Suevus" (or Swabian) is fairly common in Cologne records of the late twelfth century, but Evergeld's family can be traced from his father (fl. ca.1150) through himself and his sons Ulrich and Johann to his grandsons Heinrich Suevus and Ulrich Rufus. Evergeld was apparently the only one to hold city office although his father Ulrich does appear in a witness list of 1147, possibly as a master of Martin parish.[72] The property holdings that can be shown for the family were mostly in Martin parish.[73] Four men with the designation "Suevus" are listed in the gild list of Martin parish: Werner, Albrecht, Gottfried, and Everhart.[74] No connection can be shown between these men and the family of Evergeld Suevus, probably because the name "Suevus" was given to anyone who came to Cologne from the region of the Upper Rhine. It would not be inconsistent with the known facts about the family of Evergeld to assume that his father Ulrich had come as a merchant from that area, purchased land in

---

68. H. I, p.24 (Mart. 2 I 20). He is listed among the *seniores magistri*. H. II, pp.18, 21; *Quellen* I, p.150: *Bürgerverzeichnisse*.

69. H. I, pp.23–4 and p.23, n.2 (Mart. 2 I 13); H. I, p.29 (Mart. 2 II 21). Dowry to his wife Margaret: H. I, p.45 (Mart. 3 II 5); p.116 (Mart. 7 V 22); p.34 (Mart. 2 III 32): domum . . . sitam iuxta Renum.

70. *Quellen* I 65: Qua propter una dierum celebratis aput nos exequiis sigewini subprefecti. . . .

71. *Quellen* I, 90, 94.

72. H. I, p.23, n.2. The transaction concerns a gift of city land to the chapter at Hirsau, which was then registered in the parish registry of St. Martin. The witness list contains a number of known masters of Martin parish although there is no such designation in the document in question.

73. H. I, p.67 (Mart. 4 II 2: a house in the Old Market); p.69 (Mart. 4 II 22), p.202 (Mart. 14 II 5), p.201 (Mart. 13 IV 14: a house in the Markmannsgasse); p.106 (Mart. 7 II 5) and Planitz and Buyken, *Schreinsbücher*, no.42: a house *sub lobio*. In all cases the records indicate that the Suevus family purchased the land. Ulrich Suevus, the son of the *scabinus* Evergeld, also held some land in Severin parish: H. II, p.250 (Sev. 1 IV 6).

74. *Quellen* I, pp.148–55: *Bürgerverzeichnisse*, passim.

Cologne, and established himself there. But this must remain conjecture, especially since no concrete evidence of mercantile activity remains for the family.

Vogelo, *filius Hermanni*, is identified as a *scabinus* in 1159.[75] Vogelo's father was Hermann Canus.[76] Richwinus Canus and his brother Hermann appear frequently in witness lists in the period 1128–57.[77] Beyond the witness lists, little is known about Hermann Canus and his son Vogelo; but Richwin Canus and especially his sons Richwin and Dietrich appear frequently in the parish records of Lawrence parish. From ca.1160 to ca.1200 Richwin's sons used a property that had belonged to him, a property described as *super curiam*, that is, opposite the archbishop's residence, as security on loans.[78] It is possible, though not demonstrable, that Richwin and Dietrich moved to Rodenkirchen, a

75. *Quellen* I 74. He was also a witness to the craft gild ordinance of 1149 (von Loesch I 10) and a witness for the abbot of St. Martin in 1152 (*Quellen* I 65) and 1169 (*Quellen* I 78).

76. *Quellen* I 70, among the *burgensium honoratiores* who helped to establish the bourgeois hospital in Martin parish are listed "Richwinus Canus et Herimannus frater eius" and "Vogul filius ipsius Herimanni."

77. They are usually in lists that are unmistakably bourgeois: Lacomblet I 303 (1128); ibid., 338 (1139), where Herman appears alone under the rubric *de civitate*. *Quellen* I 51 (1142), both of them under the rubric *concives quoque nostri* (i.e., of the abbot of St. Martin) *qui maioris sunt etatis et auctoritatis*. H. I, p.35 (Mart. 2 III 37: ca.1142–56), Hermann alone as a witness for the abbot of St. Martin. *Quellen* I 116 (1139), however, identifies either them or another pair with the same names as pertaining to the *familia* of the abbey of St. Martin. If this double identification, as bourgeois and as dependents of one of the local religious foundations, is valid in this case, it would not be unusual for Cologne in the twelfth century. Lacomblet I 343 (1141) is a royal charter witnessed by the brothers along with the high *ministeriales* of the archbishop. Lacomblet I 349 (1143) and Lacomblet I 352 (1144) also include them in witness lists that are composed of *ministeriales* except for them; however, in none of these cases are they actually indicated as *ministeriales*.

78. A third son of Richwin, Pilgrim de curia, is mentioned with the other two in H. I, p.240 (Laur. 3 III 22). The entries in the Lawrence parish register from ca.1159 to ca.1172 concerning the above-mentioned property are: H. I, p.236 (Laur. 3 II 5) in which it is indicated that Hartwich, the brother of the *thelonearius* Gerhard Ungemaz lives in the house; H. I, p.237 (Laur. 3 V 9). The property had a substantial value; the brothers raised 270 m. on it at one time (Laur. 3 V 9) on the provision

village very near Cologne upriver, near the end of the twelfth century. The last entry concerning their property in Lawrence parish refers to them as *"Theodericus et Richwinus de Rodinkirchen."*[79]

Those who bear the designation "Niger" are extremely difficult to identify. It was more a personal name than a family name and cannot be taken as the designation of a *Geschlecht*. Gerhard Niger was a *scabinus* in the 1150's, and he appears in several lists of *honoratiores* or *optimates civitatis*.[80] He was chosen, along with other *scabini* and leading citizens, as an advocate by the convent of St. Maurice where his daughters were. He had given the convent half a *curtis* of land in Gunthersdorf near the city along with the daughters.[81] He can be shown to have held land also in the parishes of Gereon and Niederich. He was also frequently called by the abbot of St. Martin to act as a witness.[82] In addition, he was on the hospital board of the new hospital founded in Martin parish over the objections of the abbot of St. Martin.[83] Gerhard had a son of the same name.[84] It is difficult to ascertain whether references to Gerhard Niger after about 1160 refer to the father or to the son. It seems more likely, however, that most of them refer to the elder Gerhard, who remarried, to a woman named Elizabeth, and who is sometimes referred to as Gerhard Niger de curia because of land held in Lawrence parish near the archbishop's palace.[85]

---

that they could redeem it any year at Easter. Richwin and Dietrich also used an inn (*tabernum* or *herberge*) as security on a loan in the same period: H. I, p.237 (Laur. 3 II 7).

79. H. I, p.244 (Laur. 3 V 14: 1190–1200). Evidence from names alone is, of course, quite risky. H. I, p.257 (Laur. 4 VI 8) shows Richwin Canus, the younger, giving Archbishop Philip a property in the village of Ens in return for a prebend of 8 m. in Cologne.

80. *Quellen* I 74; Schäfer, p.4; Lacomblet I 392; *Quellen* I 65.

81. H. I, p.29 (Mart. 2 II 22). Lacomblet I 418.

82. Schäfer, p.164. These are documents dealing with lands held on feudal tenure from the abbey, not with town affairs.

83. *Quellen* I 70. For the conflict with the abbot of St. Martin: *Quellen* I 58.

84. Both are listed as witnesses in Lacomblet I 418.

85. In the period 1163–72 Gerhard Niger de curia entered into marriage with a woman named Elizabeth and gave her as his dower a property in Niederich (H. I, p.88: Nied. 4 I 6). If this refers to the elder Gerhard, then presumably it was his second marriage. That this is probably

There are also references in the parish records of St. Lawrence to Gerhard Niger *corduanus* in the latter half of the twelfth century.[86] The only connection between these references and the others is the name; thus it is impossible to assert with any assurance that Gerhard Niger, the *scabinus*, was also Gerhard Niger, the shoemaker.[87]

Albero de sancta Cecilia was a viscount by 1159 and a *scabinus* in the 1170's.[88] His brother Hubert was also a *scabinus* in the period 1159–80.[89] The only sure knowledge that we have of Albero is that he

---

the case is indicated by a reference from the Lawrence parish records (H. I, pp.229–30: Laur. 2 III 20) in which Gerhard Niger de curia, in the period 1147–65, guarantees to the sons he had of the daughter of Albero his home near the archiepiscopal precinct (*de curia*). This would suggest that the *filia Alberonis* was his first wife and Elizabeth his second. If this is accurate, then Gerhard's son was called Gerhard Luscus, and not Gerhard Niger (H. I, p.311: Scab. 2 IX 2). The alternative to this explanation would be to regard these references as pertaining to Gerhard the younger, which would make Gerhard Luscus the grandson of the first Gerhard Niger we can identify.

86. H. I, p.254 (Laur. 4 IV 25), p.256 (Laur. 4 VI 1).

87. There is no apparent connection between Gerhard Niger and the other Niger mentioned in the late twelfth and early thirteenth centuries. Albrecht Niger, roughly a contemporary of Gerhard, was an official (*senior magister*) of Martin parish (H. I, p.25: Mart 2 I 20). He held property primarily in Martin parish, among the cloth merchants (for example: H. I, pp.127–8: Mart. 8 VI 3, 4, 5, 8). The names of his children are known, but they cannot be followed after about 1200.

Pilgrim Niger also appears in town records in the early thirteenth century. He was a cloth merchant with a stall (*cubiculum*) in the cloth merchants' quarter. (H. I, p.318: Scab. 2 XIII 5: 2 cellaria integra sub eodem cubiculo in quo Pilegrimus suos vendit pannos. Scab. 2 XIII 6: contigue cubiculo Pilegrimi Nigri). His son was also a cloth merchant (*Quellen* II 138). But no connection can be shown among these various men called Niger.

88. H. II, p.293, n.6, says that he was a *scabinus* from 1149 on. This may be, but the witness list of 1149 (von Loesch I 10) does not differentiate between *scabini* and *meliores*. Albero is listed as *subcomes* in 1159 (*Quellen* I 74) and retained the designation *comes* for the rest of his life, as was usual. How long he actually served as viscount is difficult to say. He is listed as a *scabinus* and/or senator in 1171 (*Quellen* I 80) 1178 (ibid., 90) and 1180 (ibid., 94).

89. The references are the same as those in the preceding note. In 1159 (*Quellen* I 74) when Albero is listed as *subcomes*, Hubert is listed among

was a moneylender. In 1161 he loaned a certain Karl von Hönnigen (Hönnigen was a rural locality near Cologne) a total of 69m. for usufruct in the land held in pledge, which included in excess of 150 *iugera* of farmland, forest, and meadow and an entire *curtis* with a tower.[90] The family cannot be followed after these two members with the exception of Hubert's daughter, Gisela, who married into the Raitze family.

Heinrich Saphir was a *frater scabinorum* in 1178 and a *scabinus* in 1180.[91] He is also the person who held the house belonging to the abbot of St. Trond, which later became known as the Saphir House. In the charters regulating the tenure (in the year 1177) Heinrich is described as *dilectus noster* by the abbot. He owed the abbot 6m. annual rent and the right of hospitality one night a year for the abbot and twelve horses. The house was on the Rhine in Martin parish.[92] The only other piece of property that can be identified for Heinrich Saphir was also in Martin parish.[93] In the early thirteenth century a Cologne burgher named Gerhard Saphir appears in two witness lists.[94] He is not indicated as an office-holder, and there is no indication that he was a relative of Heinrich Saphir.

Gerhard de sancto Albano was a member of the *Richerzeche* about 1180.[95] His father was Hartmann de s. Albano, who was a witness to the earlier craft gild regulation of 1149.[96] The name de s. Albano

---

the *scabini*. The clearest reference to the fact that Albero and Hubert were brothers is Lacomblet I 418: Albero comes et frater eius Hubertus.

90. H. II, pp.293–4 (Scab. 1 II 1).

91. *Quellen* I 90, 94.

92. H. I, p.163 (Mart. 11 II 1); Charles Piot, ed., *Cartulaire de l'abbaye de saint-Trond* I (Brussels, 1870), no.11.

93. H. I, p.146 (Mart. 9 VI 10).

94. Lacomblet II 36; L. Korth, ed., "Liber privilegiorum maioris ecclesie Coloniensis: Der älteste Kartular des Kölner Domstiftes," *Westdeutsche Zeitschrift: Ergänzungsheft* 3 (1886), p.209.

95. Von Loesch I 13. Hoeniger, "Die älteste Urkunde," p.265, has full references on Gerhard. Lau in the appendix to his patrician genealogies in the *Kölner Stadtarchiv, Karte* 19, provides a genealogy.

96. Von Loesch I 10. Hoeniger calls him a *scabinus* on this basis; but, although the list does contain a large number of *scabini*, they are not distinguished from the *meliores*. Hartmann's son Gerhard was apparently not a *scabinus*. He is listed among the *cives*, after the *scabini*, in a witness list of 1180 (*Quellen* I 94).

would seem to indicate a residence in Alban parish, but the only property transactions recorded for the family are in Gereon parish. Hartmann bought a house and some land in Gereon from Gottfried of Neuss.[97] His son Gerhard let four *iugera* of land in the same parish to a servant of a cleric, and another son and a daughter of Hartmann also had property in Gereon.[98] Some grandsons of Gerhard held the fief of a tithe, as did other burghers, in an area near the town in the early thirteenth century.[99] All in all, the evidence that can be gathered on the de s. Albano is not impressive either for offices or for property. They cannot be followed after the first few decades of the thirteenth century. There is a slight possibility, however, that Heinrich, the son of Hartmann de s. Albano, was Heinrich Flacco, the founder of that patrician family.[100]

The Flacco family was of political importance only at the end of the twelfth century and the beginning of the thirteenth century. Heinrich Flacco was a *Bürgermeister* and a member of the *Richerzeche* ca. 1180.[101] Two of his sons, Franco and Bruno, were *scabini* in 1218.[102] After that no offices are recorded for the family although they can be followed until ca.1289. A certain Heinrich Flacco did serve as a *fideiussor* for the city of Cologne in 1263.[103] The chief residence of the family, the Flachenhaus, was in Alban parish. They later added the Flachenhof in Severin parish and the Morthof in Gereon parish to this substantial holding.[104] Heinrich Flacco and his sons, Franco, Bruno,

---

97. H. II, p.219 (Ger.1 IV 7). It is described as "domum unam et allodium."

98. H. II, p.22 (Ger. 1 V 17), p.242 (Ger. 3 VI 4).

99. *Quellen* II 1.

100. This is proposed by Hoeniger, "Die älteste Urkunde," pp.256, 265. The sons of Hartmann were named Gerhard, Hermann, and Heinrich. Heinrich Flacco is mentioned after his death as "Henricus Flacco de s. Albano," and he is the first of the Flacco family, which appears suddenly in the thirteenth century. Such circumstances are only the basis for conjecture, of course, not for proof.

101. Von Loesch I 13. References provided in Hoeniger, "Die älteste Urkunde," pp.255–6.

102. *Quellen* II 59.

103. *Quellen* II 453.

104. Hoeniger, "Die älteste Urkunde," pp.255–6; von Winterfeld, *Handel, Kapital, und Patriziat*, p.17. Also, H. II, p.241, n.2, in which

and Hermann, also held substantial property in the village of Geine, one hundred and eleven *iurnales* of allodial land and two and a half *mansi* of land held of the cathedral in Cologne. They sold all of this to the monks of the Maccabees in the time of Archbishop Adolf (1193–1205).[105] Their properties in Cologne passed for the most part to sons-in-law.[106] Hermann Flacco, the third of Heinrich's sons lent money, but the sums (15½s., 6m.) were not especially large.[107] Several men named Flacco appear in the records of the thirteenth century, but they have lost political influence. After 1289 all traces of the family are lost.[108]

Waldever Genoz is listed as a *scabinus* in the period 1178–82.[109] He was apparently dead by around 1186 since his former property in the Rheingasse in Martin parish belonged at that time (1186–88) to his son Heinrich.[110] Karl Schure is listed as a *scabinus* in 1180.[111] He held property in an area near the Rhine in Martin parish, including a

---

Hermann Flacco received the Morthof from the convent at Füssenich for an annual rent.

105. Lacomblet II 36 (1211). Fifteen *iurnales* had been recently acquired from a widow; presumably the other land had been purchased as well. The document refers to the lands in general as "bonorum sic emptorum." Apparently Heinrich had cleared or improved the land since some of it is referred to as "novales allodii." " . . . predia et allodia et agrorum culturas . . . apud villam que dicitur Geine, videlicet in allodio nonaginta et sex iurnales; nouales allodii vendiderunt etiam et ibidem, duos mansos et dimidium spectantes ad ecclesiam s. Petri in Colonia. Insuper emit a quadam vidua nomine Agnete et eius heredibus in predicta villa quindecim iurnales pro vinginti marcis. . . . " If they paid 20 m. for fifteen *iurnales* and sold the whole 111 *iurnales* and two and one-half *mansi* to the monastery of the Maccabees for 40 m., presumably they also received some religious consideration for their efforts.

106. Von Winterfeld, *Handel, Kapital, und Patriziat*, p.17.

107. H. II, p.313 (Scab. 2 X 4); Planitz and Buyken, *Schreinsbücher*, no.513.

108. Von Winterfeld, *Handel, Kapital, und Patriziat*, p.17, states that they did not lose their fortune nor did they pass into the nobility. What the basis for her statements is I do not know.

109. *Quellen* I 90, 94; H. I, p.164, n.1.

110. H. I, p.172 (Mart. 11 VI 2): domum et aream in platea Reni sitam, que fuit Waldeveri (Genoz).

111. *Quellen* I 94.

wharf.[112] Gottfried von Staveren is mentioned as a *scabinus* in 1159.[113] Staveren is a village in Frisia. Certainly Cologne had had commercial contact with this area since the early Middle Ages. Perhaps Gottfried came from there, although all conclusions based on unsupported evidence from names is risky. There is no record of Gottfried's property holdings or of any descendants although a Hermann von Staveren is mentioned as a *scabinus* in 1178.[114] Hermann de sancto Mauritio was a member of the *Richerzeche* ca.1180. His father-in-law was Ludwig von Mummersloch, and he held property in Martin and Lawrence parishes. He had a son of the same name, and after that the family cannot be followed.[115]

Ten men can be identified as *scabini* in the twelfth century, but beyond that nothing is known about them. They are Hermann *Ditwigis filius* and Gottfried *Volfuendis filius, scabini* in 1159;[116] Vugelo *comes, scabinus* in 1176;[117] Karl Sairo, Franco Parvus, Gerhard *filius Richolfi, scabini* in 1178;[118] Franco de strata lapidea (possibly the same as Franco Parvus) and Hermann *thelonearius, scabini* in 1180;[119] Antonius, *scabinus* in 1171;[120] and Bruno *frater Malbodonis*, a citizen of

---

112. H. I, p.146 (Mart. 9 VI 7).

113. *Quellen* I 74. In the general period 1150–80 there are direct references to his activity as a *scabinus* rendering judgment in court alone in the name of the other *scabini*: H. II, p.298 (Scab. I V 1,3). He also appears in four witness lists of the abbot of St. Martin between 1145 and 1169. In three of these he is among obvious *scabini* and burghers (1145: *Quellen* I 54; 1152: ibid., 65; 1169: ibid., 78). The 1152 list, which includes Gottfried, ends "aliique conplures de optimatibus huius ciuitatis," and that designation fits the identifiable witnesses very well. The fourth list (1145: *Quellen* I 55) drawn up in the name of the abbot of St. Martin, ends, "et alii de familia nostra quam plurimi." Except for Gottfried, none of the names is familiar among the officeholders in Cologne at this time. Perhaps Gottfried was a member of the *familia* of St. Martin.

114. *Quellen* I 90.

115. Hoeniger, "Die älteste Urkunde," p.267.

116. *Quellen* I 74.

117. Lacomblet I 455.

118. *Quellen* I 90.

119. *Quellen* I 94.

120. *Quellen* I 81. He also can be shown to have acted alone as a representative of the *scabini* in maintaining the peace: H. II, p.298 (Scab. 1 V 2).

Martin parish, and a *scabinus* in 1169 and 1178.[121]

These men, from the Ungemaz, about whom we know a great deal, to the last ten *scabini*, about whom we know nothing, comprise the majority of the twelfth-century leaders who can be identified; but a second group is even more important for our purposes. These are men who founded true *Geschlechter*, men prominent in the twelfth century who prepared the way for the patrician families of the Jude, Raitze, von Mummersloch, Grin, Scherfgin, Parfuse, von Mühlengassen, Cleingedank, and of Waldever the *Vogt*.

Werner, the first known member of the Jude family, was a *thelonearius* in Cologne and, apparently, a *ministerialis*.[122] His son Daniel was also a *thelonearius* until the reform of the Cologne *Tafelgüter* (properties pertaining to the daily or charitable needs of the archbishop) in 1152. Until that time father and son apparently held the toll at Cologne in fief from the archbishop.[123] Werner held property in Martin parish.[124]

Werner had three important sons, Bruno, Daniel, and Alexander. All three were *scabini*, and Daniel, as mentioned, was a *thelonearius* after his father, until 1152.[125] Both Bruno and Daniel were dead by about

---

121. Beyer, et al., *Urkundenbuch . . . mittelrheinischen Territorien* I 658 (1169); Lacomblet I 464 (1178). Bruno also acted alone as a representative of the *scabini*: H. II, p.298 (Scab. 1 V 2). He was a citizen of the Martin parish, quite possibly a parish master there: H. I, p.35, n.1; H. II, p.298, n.3.

122. Lacomblet I 300 (1125). He is listed among the *ministeriales* of the archbishop; however, the document was a grant of toll privileges at Cologne for the merchants of Siegburg, and Werner was no incidental witness. He is described as "Wernherus tunc coloniensis thelonearius qui et tunc presens fuit et hoc fieri expetit." Genealogical information on the family is provided by Lau, *Mitteilungen* 26, pp.115—9.

123. Lacomblet I 375. See above, Chapter 4, n.64. Arnold II of Cologne, a former royal chancellor, was elected in 1151 after a period of troubles in the archdiocese. He recollected the properties which had been granted in fief since the time of Archbishop Frederick I (1099—1131) and which pertained to the *mensa* or the *elemosina* of the archbishop. The toll at Cologne seems to be the central concern. The properties are described in the summation as "teloneum urbis colonie et multa episcopalia servicia."

124. H. I, p.16 (Mart. 1 II 10) where Werner is called *dominus*; ibid., p.17 (Mart. 1 IV 2). Both entries are from the earliest period of the Martin parish register (ca.1135—42).

125. Lacomblet I 403; P. Joerres, ed., *Urkundenbuch des Stiftes St.*

1170; Alexander lived for at least another decade after that. Bruno's wife, Richmud, remarried to Conrad von Burgele, a prominent *minsterialis* whose family had close ties to the town. The town land recorded for Daniel and Bruno was all in Martin parish and included, besides a house on the Rheingasse and another in the market, typical properties such as market stalls, a granary, a bakehouse, and a garden.[126]

Many prominent burghers of the twelfth and thirteenth centuries acquired land in the country. Daniel and Bruno held twelve *iurnales* of land in Dünwald from the provost of the cathedral and twelve *iurnales* in the same village from the provost of St. Gereon in Cologne. This property was held in benefice without the payment of a rent although the brothers did grant a vineyard in Remagen to St. Gereon, which paid six casks of wine a year and which was supposed to guarantee the brothers "safe possession" of their benefice. Around 1160 the brothers sold their benefices to the nuns at Dünwald, and the land was converted to censual land with charges of a yearly rent and a payment to each new administrator of the *curia* of which the lands were a part. The *mansum* and the four *iurnales* at Pafferode, which the brothers held for rents respectively of 6s. and 4 *nummi*, were also sold to the sisters at Dünwald.[127] It is not known why the brothers, or presumably their father, should have received benefices from these churches. One possibility might be that they were rewards for Werner's and Daniel's

---

Gereon zu Köln (Bonn, 1893) no.17. Both come from about 1160 and mention Daniel and Bruno as the sons of Werner *thelonearius*. As *scabini*: *Quellen* I 74 for Daniel and Bruno; ibid. 94 for Alexander. They are listed together among the *optimates civitatis* in *Quellen* I 65. Daniel as *thelonearius*: H. I, p.29 (Mart. 2 II 22 where Daniel *thelonearius* along with five other prominent city leaders was made an advocate for the sisters of St. Maurice, to protect their city properties.

126. References to Daniel, the son of Bruno, his mother Richmud, and his guardian Alexander (presumably his uncle) in the period 1168—72: H. I, p.94 (Mart. 6 II 5) p.102 (Mart. 7 I 7). References to the disposition of Daniel's properties: H. I, p.54 (Mart 3 V 3), p.112 (Mart. 7 IV 2), p.115 (Mart. 7 V 15) from the period 1171—2. Daniel died without heirs apparently since his property went to the church (St. Maria in Künigsdorf) where his sister was a nun and to his nephew Daniel. The parish registry entries mention Richmud as the wife of Conrad von Burgele as early as 1171—2: H. I, p.54 (Mart. 3 V 2).

127. Lacomblet I 403; Joerres, *Urkundenbuch . . . St. Gereon*, 17. The record is not completely clear on exactly which land was held from which church.

service as *thelonearii*. The vineyards in Remagen may well indicate some connection to the wine trade, but the striking feature of the properties is their diversification: some general farmland, some vineyards, some market land, including a possible connection with milling operations, and income from the city toll.

The first member of the family to use the surname "Jude" was Daniel, that son of Bruno and Richmud mentioned before. In that sense he is the founder of the Jude family.[128] It is possible that the family was Jewish in origin; recent converts appear as parish magistrates and other prominent burghers in the twelfth century.[129] But it is more likely that "Jude" was a nickname like Gir (*avarus*) or Cleingedank (*parvi mentes*). It was not adopted until the third generation of those family members whom we can identify, and it agrees well with the tendency to make fun of greed.[130] Daniel Jude, like his father and uncles, was a *scabinus*,[131] and the Jude continued to be represented in the scabinal college, the *Richerzeche*, and the town council throughout the thirteenth century. Probably the most prominent member of the family was Daniel Jude, a grandson of the first Daniel Jude. Although exiled from the town in 1260 during the patrician wars, he was a *scabinus* and *Bürgermeister* in the 1280's when the Overstolz faction, with which the Jude family was allied, won. Daniel Jude had a reputation as one of the richest men in Cologne. He became a vassal of the bishop of Liége and from that time on was designated as a knight, a not uncommon occurrence in thirteenth-century Cologne.[132] The family remained prominent in Cologne until the late seventeenth century.[133]

The family name Raitze derives from a Cologne burgher of the early twelfth century named Razo. Although certain identification cannot be made, this was probably Razo of Suphtele, a village near Kempen on the

128. His uncle Daniel died without heirs. Lau, *Mitteilungen* 26, p.117, also lists no heirs for his uncle Alexander.

129. The most prominent case is that of the de s. Laurentio, already discussed.

130. Lau, *Mitteilungen* 26, p.115, leans to the view that Jude was a *Spottname*.

131. *Quellen* II 59 (1218).

132. Lau, *Mitteilungen* 26, pp.115, 118; von Winterfeld, *Handel, Kapital, und Patriziat*, pp.15–6.

133. Ibid., p.16.

Lower Rhine, who was a *ministerialis* of St. Pantaleon.[134] Razo appears as a witness for the city in an early record of a land transaction.[135] Hermann, the son of Razo, was a *ministerialis* of St. Pantaleon and a *scabinus* in the period 1149–59.[136] Hermann's son Heinrich Razo is listed as a *scabinus* in the period 1167–88, appears as a member of the *Richerzeche* in the first extant document of that group (ca.1179–82), and is listed as a *ministerialis* of the archbishop in a document of 1195.[137] Heinrich lived in the market area of Martin parish together with his wife Gisela, who was a daughter of Hupert, the brother of the viscount Albero de s. Cecilia.[138] He also held land in Gereon parish and allodial property in the village of Hönnigen near Cologne.[139]

---

134. Lau, *Mitteilungen* 26, pp.137–8, provides a genealogy of the Raitze family. He identifies both Razo and his son Hermann as *ministeriales* of St. Pantaleon. Hoeniger, "Die älteste Urkunde," p.261, n.3, thinks it more likely that the original Razo was a burgher of Lawrence parish and a member of the merchant gild; however, Hoeniger himself admits that the two Razos may, in fact, be one man. It was not uncommon in the twelfth century for a man to be both a *ministerialis* of a church and a burgher at the same time. The reference Lau found to Hermann the son of Razo as a *ministerialis* of St. Pantaleon (Alfter 14, p.215: 1158) makes this most likely. Hoeniger does not cite this reference, perhaps because the collection in which it appeared was in large part outdated by later collections. He does give the references to Razo of Suphtele as a *ministerialis* (Lacomblet I 303,363; ibid. IV 618, 620). In addition to the references given by Lau and Hoeniger, Razo appears as a witness in a list that is unlabeled, but almost entirely ministerial; the list concerns the *familia* of Suphtele among others: Lacomblet I 349 (1143).

135. *Quellen* I 43 (ca.1120–4). That he is listed under the rubric *de civitate* is not surprising since the church referred to in the other rubric (*ministri ecclesie*) was either St. Severin or the cathedral. The document appears to be a very early record of a transaction since the customary parish authorities are missing. This has led Hoeniger to speculate that the burghers listed might be *scabini*.

136. Full references in Lau, *Mitteilungen* 26, p.138, and Hoeniger, "Die älteste Urkunde," p.261, n.2.

137. Ibid.; von Loesch I 13; Lacomblet I 547.

138. H. II, p.310 (Scab. 2 VII 4): Heinrich Razo and his wife grant to their son Dietrich one half "domus que sita est in foro in qua (Henricus et Gysela) manserunt."

139. H. II, p.293 (Scab. 1 I 2), p.305 (Scab. 2 V 2) in which Hermann, the son of Heinrich Razo, grants to his wife "curiam cum domibus et areis

The most important line of the Raitze was descended from Heinrich's son Dietrich. His grandson, also named Dietrich, was a *Bürgermeister* in 1272, a *scabinus*, a knight, and an active participant in the patrician wars. Of Dietrich's three sons all were knights and two were *scabini* at the end of the thirteenth century; one was a member of the town council and a member of the *Richerzeche* in the early fourteenth century.[140] In the fourteenth century the family moved into the local nobility. Dietrich Raitze, the *Bürgermeister*, had married the daughter of a local landed family; their children also married well. By the end of the fourteenth century, the family had virtually disappeared from Cologne and had been established in the local landed society.[141]

The von Mummersloch family can be traced back to a Ludwig von Mummersloch who died around 1165 or 1170.[142] Around that time Ludwig's widow granted her son Dietrich some property (*predium . . . in silva et in campis*) in Merheim near Cologne.[143] Ludwig presumably lived in Alban parish in the house "Mummersloch," which is probably the source of the family name. He also had property in Martin parish.[144] No offices are known for Ludwig, but his sons rose to prominence in the town. His son Ludwig is mentioned as a *scabinus* many times between 1167 and 1182; he was also a member of the *Richerzeche*.[145] Another son Dietrich is mentioned as a *scabinus* in 1178 and 1180.[146]

---

in Hoingin cum allodio, sicut ipse et pater suus et mater sua in propria possessione possederant."

140. Lau, *Mitteilungen* 26, p.137.

141. Von Winterfeld, *Handel, Kapital, und Patriziat*, p.10.

142. A genealogy with full references appears in Lau, *Mitteilungen* 26, pp.130–3.

143. H. II, p.295 (Scab. 1 III 3).

144. Lau, *Mitteilungen* 26, p.130, on the derivation of the name. The Mummersloch area in Alban parish was already a large complex in the twelfth century: von Winterfeld, *Handel, Kapital, und Patriziat*, p.18. In the period 1135–42 Ludwig and his wife granted a house in Martin parish to their daughter and son-in-law Dietrich and then sold it to Dietrich's parents: H. I, p.19 (Mart. 1 V 3). Cf. also H. I, p.176 (Mart. 12 I 5) where Ludwig's children have clearly inherited from him a house located *super aqueductum* in Martin parish.

145. Hoeniger, "Die älteste Urkunde," p.256, has assembled all the references. Von Loesch I 13 indicates that Ludwig de Mimbirsloche was an official of the *Richerzeche* ca.1180.

146. *Quellen* I 90, 91; Lacomblet III 474.

A third son Heinrich was a *Schultheiss* for the abbot of St. Martin in the village of Flittard near Cologne.[147] This is the only indication of a *ministerialis* status for a member of the von Mummersloch family. The only sure evidence of mercantile activity for a member of the family concerns a member of the cloth merchants' gild in the early fourteenth century; nevertheless, circumstantial evidence does seem to indicate mercantile activity in the family in the twelfth century.[148]

In a series of grants in the late twelfth and early thirteenth century, Ludwig von Mummersloch divided his property among his children. At least eight different houses, a garden, and a market stand are mentioned in various parts of the city, and this does not include bequests made to two of his sons, Ludwig and Dietrich (the latter of whom took the name de Pavone) who were prominent men in Cologne.[149] Ludwig frequently made loans, usually for modest sums (6m. for one year; 30m.

---

147. H. I, p.164, n.1 (1182). The document concerns a house in Cologne belonging to the abbey of St. Martin. Heinrich appears in the witness list among the abbey officials and before the *scabini*: Henricus frater Ludewici de Minsbernslogus tunc temporis scultetus in Vlitard. The position of *Schultheiss* in Flittard was not hereditary at this time. It had almost escaped the grasp of the abbot in the mid-twelfth century, but he had managed to prevent it from becoming hereditary. Cf. *Quellen* I 55 (1145), 56 (1143), 65 (1152).

148. Lau, *Mitteilungen* 26, p.131, mentions a Richolf von Mummersloch who was a member of the *Gewandschneider*. He belongs to a branch of the family (probably) that Lau could not establish in the main genealogy. Von Winterfeld, *Handel, Kapital, und Patriziat* pp.18-19, thinks mercantile interests are obvious for the von Mummersloch family; however, possession of market property does not make one a merchant. Nor is it sufficient to assert that a strict *commercium* and *connubium* was the rule among the cloth merchants. The evidence is more convincing for the fourteenth century (ibid., pp.20−1), but there is no reason to think that a family including cloth merchants in the fourteenth century need necessarily have included cloth merchants in the twelfth century. The property of the von Mummersloch will be considered below, but another bit of evidence which von Winterfeld includes (as always, without a reference) is that Hermann von Mummersloch, the son of the *scabinus* and *Richerzeche* member Ludwig, settled a conflict between the Count of Altena and the burghers of Bremen around 1200. While this does not "prove" he was a long-distance trader, it, together with the other circumstances, makes it appear likely.

149. H. II, p.122 (Nied. 8 IV 20), p.169 (Nied. 11 VIII 25), pp.300−1 (Scab. 2 II 2−6).

for seven and one-half years) for which he typically received a house or market stall as security. There is also a record that he lent one hundred measures of grain to a certain Karl (possibly Karl the *thelonearius*).[150] The main lines of the von Mummersloch family were founded by the sons of Ludwig, who died in the early thirteenth century.[151] Beginning with his son Dietrich de Pavone (von der Poe), a number of his descendants were *scabini,* and by 1305 his greatgrandson Thilmann de Pavone was a member of the town council.[152] The von Mummersloch also held an advocate's court *(Vogteigericht)* in a special district of the city called Eigelstein. Eigelstein was an area closely dependent on the archbishop and the area where his prison was located. The von Mummersloch held the jurisdiction in fief until 1324 when the archbishop bought it back from them. By the end of the fourteenth century the influence of the von Mummersloch had disappeared.[153]

Men with the surname Grin were *scabini* in the twelfth, thirteenth, and fourteenth centuries in Cologne, as well as members of the *Richerzeche* and of the town council. There were so many burghers with the name Grin that it is impossible to establish one genealogy for them

---

150. H. I, p.58 (Mart. 3 VI 9), p.117 (Mart. 8 I 3), p.120 (Mart. 8 II 7), p.123 (Mart. 8 III 6), p.188 (Mart. 12 V 15). Typically the properties used for security were in Martin parish. This fact would not make Ludwig a merchant anymore than his scattered holding in the rest of the city made him a landed gentleman. Yet von Winterfeld, *Handel, Kapital, und Patriziat*, p.19, insists: "In seinen Geldleihgeschäften, die sich einmal auf Weizenlieferung erstreckten, bevorzugte er als Pfand Verkaufsstände, Hallen, und Wandschneidertische. Hieraus und aus dem Beruf seiner Enkel und Urenkel lässt sich folgern, dass er Tuchhändler war."

Ludwig bought one *mensa* (H. I, p.186: Mart 12 IV 14) and received one as a pledge on a loan (H. I, p.188: Mart 12 V 15). This is the extent of his property that was undeniably mercantile. Does this mean that he "preferred" such property as security on a loan? And, even if it does or if some of the other property was used as shops, does this make Ludwig a merchant? The connection is not proved. The grandson and the great-grandson of Ludwig that von Winterfeld mentions may have been cloth merchants, but she gives no sources, and Lau could only find one cloth merchant in the family, and he could not establish a family relationship between him (Richolf von Mummersloch) and Ludwig!

151. He was dead by about 1205–14: Lau, *Mitteilungen* 26, p.132.

152. Ibid., pp.132–3.

153. Von Winterfeld, *Handel, Kapital, und Patriziat*, pp.18, 20.

all.[154] The name Grin also appears among the *ministeriales* and *milites* of the archbishop in the thirteenth century. It is usually assumed that these persons represent yet another branch of the family, which entered the archbishop's service, although this cannot be demonstrated. In fact, it may be that the name was derived separately by different families.[155]

At least five men named Grin appear in the Cologne records in the latter half of the twelfth century. The earliest reference is to Ludolf Grin, who was a witness in the gild regulation document of 1149 and probably was a *scabinus*.[156] It is not known whether Ludolf is an ancestor of any of the later Grins, but Vugelo Grin, the "founder" of one of the five lines identified by Lau, was a *frater scabinorum* in 1178. He had property in Lawrence and Niederich parishes.[157] Also in the witness list of 1178, which includes Ludolf Grin as a *scabinus* and Vugelo Grin as a *frater scabinorum*, is Gottfried "the son of Ludolf" as a *frater scabinorum*. This may well be Gottfried Grin. Gottfried Grin appears as a resident of Niederich parish and a parish magistrate of Lawrence parish

---

154. Lau, *Mitteilungen* 25, pp.378—81, provides the genealogies for the family. He identifies five separate lines, most of which can be traced only back to ca.1200, and a number of other persons who do not fit into these five lines. What relation these thirteenth- and fourteenth-century lines may have to the persons named Grin in the twelfth century is not known, but some connection is probable.

155. Dietrich Grin as a *ministerialis: Quellen* II 59 (1218); Reiner Grin as a knight and probably as a castellan in Lechenich: Richard Knipping, ed., *Die Regesten der Erzbischöfe von Köln im Mittelalter* III, pt.2 (Bonn, 1913) 2314 (1264) and Lacomblet II 432 (1256). If you put these two, who do not fit into Lau's genealogies, together with the great number of Grins in Cologne and with a certain Peter Grin, who was the archbishop's contested candidate for canon of St. Paul's in Trier in the 1280's (Knipping, *Regesten* III, 2, no.2310; J. Guirard, ed., *Les Registres d'Urbain IV* (Paris, 1899—1904), III 1985) you can either conclude that the one family was extremely widespread or that there were in fact two or more families with the same name. Both Lau, *Mitteilungen* 25, p.378, and von Winterfeld, *Handel, Kapital, und Patriziat*, p.26, assume that the ministerial line split off in the twelfth century.

156. Von Loesch I 10; *Quellen* I 90. A Ludolf Grin was also a witness for the abbess of St. Maria in Capitolio in 1193 (Schäfer, "Inventare und Regesten," *Annalen* 71 (1901), p.41). Considering the time span, there may well have been two Ludolf Grins.

157. *Quellen* I 90. H. II, p.117 (Nied. 8 I 9); Lau, *Mitteilungen* 25, p.378.

in the late twelfth century.[158] The fourth of the five men named Grin to appear in the twelfth century was Richwin Grin, the "founder" of another of Lau's five lines. No offices are recorded for him, but he had property in Niederich, Columba, and Gereon parishes.[159] He also held the fief of a tithe in an area (Sülz) near the town and was a witness in 1203 to a document concerning the privileges of the merchants of Dinant in Cologne.[160] The fifth twelfth-century Grin was Richolf Grin, who held property on the banks of the Rhine in Niederich.[161] He cannot be related to the genealogies either. Despite our fragmentary knowledge of the Grin family in the twelfth century, it is worth noting that no property is recorded as belonging to any of them in Martin parish. Their major holdings were in Columba, Lawrence, and especially Niederich parishes. That they did not hold at least some market land made them unusual.

The Grin family becomes too numerous and too fragmented to follow fully in the thirteenth century. All five lines were of equal prominence.[162] Grins fought on both sides in the patrician wars. Cooperation with the Weisen against the Overstolz meant the fall from prominence of a couple of lines, but in general the family maintained itself well into the fourteenth century. In addition to offices, such as *scabinus*, *Bürgermeister*, and town councilor, one line held the market toll in fief from the *Stadtvogt* and the chamberlain in the latter half of the

---

158. *Quellen* I 90. Godefridus filius Lodolfi appears in the witness list directly after Vugelo Grin. He may have been the son of some other Ludolf, of course, but it was generally customary for the *fratres scabinorum* to be relatives of the *scabini*. Niederich residence: H II, p.84 (Nied. 3 III 8). As a parish magistrate in Lawrence: H. I, p.261 (Laur. 4 IX 4). He and Gerhard Ungemaz received a surety for the whole body of magistrates guaranteeing the effestucation of a minor heir.

159. H. II, p.135 (Nied. 9 VI 16, 17), p.136 (Nied. 9 VII 14), p.167 (Nied. 11 VII 19); Lau, *Mitteilungen* 25, p.379.

160. *Quellen* II 1: pheodum unum prefate decime tenuit Rigwinus Grien, quod fuit Hermanni uenditoris lane. *Quellen* II 5: Richwin may well have been a *scabinus* since this list includes a number of known *scabini*, but the witnesses are not identified by title.

161. H. II, p.169 (Nied. 11 IX 4).

162. It is possible that Richwin Grin (founder of line 1) and Berwin Grin (founder of line 3) were brothers. Cf. H. II, p.135 (Nied. 9 VI 17) and p.167 (Nied. 11 VII 19) where Berwin is called Berwinus de s. Columba.

thirteenth century and in the fourteenth century until 1379, when it was bought back.[163]

How deeply they may have been involved in commerce is as difficult to say for the Grin family as it is for most of the other patrician families. They had few ties with Martin parish and cannot be shown as merchants until the fourteenth century when two Grins are mentioned as members of the drapers' gild and one as a member of the woad merchants' gild.[164]

The first recorded members of the Scherfgin family are Hermann and his relative (*cognatus*) Gottfried, both of whom were *fratres scabinorum* in 1178 and *scabini* in 1180.[165] Hermann Scherfgin lived on the market

---

163. Von Winterfeld, *Handel, Kapital, und Patriziat*, p.28.

164. Von Loesch I 95 (1344): Herman Grijn Kreich and Herman Grijn der Kale as "unverdiente" members of the gild, that is members who have not served as officials of the gild. The descent of neither man can be established in Lau's genealogies, which end in 1325 in any case. Von Loesch I 110A (first half of the fourteenth century: Hermannus Grin de Aldenb. . . . The rest of the name is illegible. Possibly this is Hermann Grin de Antiqua Ursa (von Aldenbären?) a member of the fifth line established by Lau (no.159 in his genealogy). Von Winterfeld, *Handel, Kapital, und Patriziat*, p.30, states that the Grin cannot be shown as merchants: "Als Kaufleute lassen sich die Grin, die unter den Münzerhausgenossen gut vertreten waren, nicht nachweisen." Yet indications of mercantile activity seem no worse—and no better— than those of other families she positively identifies as merchants; that is, circumstances such as wealth, dealing in land, moneylending, marriages to mercantile families, etc., and identification as merchants in the fourteenth century. Of course, in the passage just indicated, von Winterfeld still claims the Grin for the merchants, chiefly because one or two of them married merchants' daughters.

165. *Quellen* I 90, 94. Lau, *Mitteilungen* 26, pp.139–41, gives genealogical data on the two main lines of the family up to 1325. There are a number of other men identified as Serfwin, Scerfwin, Scheverken, etc., in the twelfth-century records, but their relationship, if any, to the rest of the family cannot be established. Conrad Scerfwin or Serfwin appears in the gild lists of St. Martin (H. II, pt.2, pp.24, 48). There were two, possibly three, Gerhard Scerfwins or Scheverchens in the late twelfth century, either of whom may be the ancestor of the second line of the family identified by Lau. Gerhard Skerfwin, brother of Richolf: H. I, p.334 (Col. 1 III 10), p.339 (Col. 1 VI 14), p.343 (Col. 1 IX 9, 10), p.350 (Col. 1 XIII 22), p.372 (Col. 2 XIII 24). Gerhard Schervechen, son of Dietrich and brother of Gottfried (the *cognatus* of Hermann?): H. II, p.64 (Nied. 1 XI 7), p.106 (Nied. 6 III 19). Gerhard Schervechen, married to

and owned several market stalls and halls.[166] Some of the property, at least, had belonged to his father Richolf the Younger and his grandfather Richolf the Elder as well.[167] Gottfried Scherfgin also lived on the market; he had an area in Niederich and appears in the records as a moneylender.[168] The second line of the Scherfgin family cannot be followed until the thirteenth century. In the thirteenth and fourteenth centuries both branches of the family had the usual complement of *scabini*, town councilors, members of the *Richerzeche*, and knights.

The thirteenth-century Scherfgin about whom we know the most is Gerhard Scherfgin, a grandson of Hermann. He was the patron of Gottfried Hagen, who describes him as a great bourgeois knight. He did hold fiefs from the archbishop and a number of great lords in the area of the Lower Rhine, and most of his landed wealth was not in the town; but he seems to have maintained an interest in business. He is mentioned as a cloth merchant in Brussels in 1270, and some of his duties for the archbishop early in his life (1219–27) had been dealing with the archbishop's debtors in Rome and at the French fairs. He was a *scabinus* in Cologne as well.[169] The importance of the Scherfgin continued well into the fourteenth century.

Liverad instead of Christina (a second marriage or a different Gerhard?): H. II, p.152 (Nied. 10 X 14).

166. Hermann's dower to his wife Irmingard mentions two houses and several halls in Martin: H. I, pp.183–4 (Mart. 12 III 4–7, 9). Hermann apparently granted most of the property out on a lifetime tenure for an annual rent: H. I, p.123 (Mart. 8 III 14), p.125 (Mart. 8 V 5, 6), p.162 (Mart. 11 I 20). Possibly Hermann himself used one of the stalls for business, but the "ipse" in the following seems to apply to Albert rather than to Hermann since the later use of "ipse" in the same passage only makes sense when applied to Albert: H. I, p.118 (Mart. 8 I 13): ... Hermannus filius Ricolfi Iuvenis exposuit Alberto filio Warneri statiunculam in foro in qua ipse stat pro 13 marc. a festo s. Petri in augusto ad annum, prout, si tunc eam non redimat, ipse annuatim eam pro lucro (sine censu) donec eam redimat. . . .

167. H. I, p.56 (Mart. 3 V 31).

168. H. I, p.307 (Brig. 3 I 2); H. II, p.106 (Nied. 6 III 19); H. I, p.80 (Mart. 5 I 7).

169. Von Winterfeld, *Handel, Kapital, und Patriziat* pp.47–8, describes his career. Cf. also Lau, *Mitteilungen* 26, p.139; *Quellen* II 196 (his testament); *Hansisches Urkundenbuch* I 677 (his business relations with Brussels).

The name Parfuse first appears in Cologne records in the 1170's with Richolf Parfuse, a *scabinus* and a member of the *Richerzeche*.[170] Richolf Parfuse is probably identical with Richolf Sparwer, who appears as a witness in 1152 (in a list primarily of *scabini*) and in 1157 (in a list of *burgensium honoratiores*).[171] Richolf's parents were probably Bertradis von der Mühlengassen and a certain Rainer of Basel.[172] His brothers were probably Rainer de Barba in *platea molendinorum* and Hermann and Conrad Minnevuz, who have already been discussed.

---

170. Lau drew up a genealogy of the Parfuse with references, which is in the *Kölner Stadtarchiv* as an appendix to his published genealogies, *Karte* 12. In the early phases, however, it is confused and almost surely wrong. Hoeniger, "Die älteste Urkunde," pp.262–3, gives full references for Richolf Parfuse.

171. The identity of the "two" men, suggested by Hoeniger, ibid., p.262, n.3, is made probable by a comparison of two entries in the Niederich parish records. H. II, p.114 (Nied. 7 V 13) records that "Richolfus qui dicitur Sparewere" acquired a house "que erat Berwini et Gertrudis" from their children. A later entry (H. II, p.116: Nied. 8 I 1) records that all the heirs of Richolf and of Berwin sold the "patrimonium (domum in Snegilgazzen) quod fuit Berwini et uxoris sue Gertrudis, quod venerat in proprietatem Richolfi Parfusi et uxoris sue Gertrudis." It appears likely, then, that Richolf Parfuse and Richolf Sparwer are the same man.

It is not likely, however, that Richolf Parfuse (Sparwer) was ever the subadvocate of the city. A Richolf Sporger is listed as subadvocate in 1149 (von Loesch I 10) and a Richolfus advocatus is mentioned several times in the period 1145–69 (e.g., *Quellen* I 54, 65, 78, 117; H. II, p.293: Scab. 1 I 2). But in 1152 (*Quellen* I 65) both Richolfus advocatus and Richolfus Sparwer are listed as witnesses. It would still be possible to imagine circumstances in which Richolf Parfuse could have been subadvocate, but it must appear highly unlikely. This goes against Lau's conclusions in the genealogy mentioned above and in *Die erbischöflichen Beamten im 12. Jahrhundert*, p.73, as well as those of von Winterfeld, *Handel, Kapital, und Patriziat*, p.9. Hoeniger, "Die älteste Urkunde," p.263, pointed out the inconsistency of regarding Richolf Parfuse (Sparwer) as a subadvocate.

172. H. I, p.118 (Mart. 8 I 16): Richolfo Parfuse et matre eius Bertrade; H. I, p.129 (Mart. 8 VI 21): Bertradis de platea molendinorum et filius eius Ricolfus. Both entries concern the leasing of market stalls though the two entries do not seem to refer to the same stall. Rainer was the husband of Bertrad; he was dead by ca.1150–5 (Hoeniger, "Die älteste Urkunde," p.263, n.1). Von Winterfeld, *Handel, Kapital, und Patriziat*, p.8, identifies him as Rainer von Basel.

Richolf Parfuse lived in the Mühlengasse in Brigida parish. He dealt in property in several areas of the city, including a number of market stalls.[173] As one of his many land deals, Richolf acquired a property in Columba parish called Berlich. Using this as a nucleus, his son, also named Richolf Parfuse, built up a substantial holding with vineyards and orchards (what is called a *curia* or *Hof* in the records) in which he lived. To complete his impressive holding, the younger Richolf received the adjacent Roman tower as an hereditary fief from the count of Holland.[174]

The elder Richolf had three children of whom records remain: Richolf, Constantine, and Bertradis, who was married to a subadvocate named Emund. Richolf, the one who built up the property in Berlich, and his descendants were the most important. He was a *scabinus* and a *Bürgermeister*.[175] Both Richolf and his brother Constantine are mentioned as *ministeriales* of the archbishop in 1208.[176] Richolf's son Werner (d. 1276) was a knight who played an important part in the patrician wars of the thirteenth century and, as a consequence, damaged the standing of the family in the town. There was still a Parfuse as viscount in 1292, but the family disappears in the fourteenth century.[177]

The first member of the von Mühlengassen or Weise family of whom we have knowledge is the *Bürgermeister* Dietrich von Mühlengassen, who is mentioned ca.1180 as an official of the *Richerzeche*.[178] Many of his sons, grandsons, and great-grandsons were *scabini*; in the first half of the

---

173. Hoeniger, "Die älteste Urkunde," p.262, gives the references.

174. Von Winterfeld, *Handel, Kapital, und Patriziat*, p.9 on the tower: H. II, p.317 (Scab. 2 XII 8); the tower is described as a *propugnaculum* or *wichus*.

175. As a *scabinus: Quellen* II 59 (1218). He and his brother Constantine were frequently witnesses in the early thirteenth century. These witness lists may be lists of *scabini*, but they are not designated as such. Cf. *Quellen* II 29 (1205–8) 49 (1215); Knipping, "Ungedruckte Urkunden," p.186. Von Winterfeld, *Handel, Kapital, und Patriziat*, p.9, identifies him as a *Bürgermeister* in 1216.

176. Knipping, *Die Regesten*, III, Personen- und Ortsregister, p.395.

177. Von Winterfeld, *Handel, Kapital, und Patriziat*, pp.9–10.

178. Von Loesch I 13. Hoeniger, "Die älteste Urkunde," p.255, provides the relevant information on Dietrich. Genealogical data for the family is given by Lau, *Mitteilungen* 26, pp.126–9.

thirteenth century the family dominated the scabinal college. One son and one great-grandson were *Bürgermeister*.[179]

The first Dietrich von Mühlengassen lived in Brigida parish, where he possessed substantial mercantile property. He also acquired property in Martin and Holy Apostles parishes.[180] Of Dietrich's three sons, two, Gottfried Rufus and Ludwig, were also residents of Brigida parish.[181] Ludwig inherited the property in Apostles parish and acquired, through inheritance or otherwise, an entire mill on the river.[182] The third son, Dietrich, married the daughter of a prominent family in Niederich parish and established himself there on property obtained from his wife's family. In fact, he appears to have had his house built for him and his wife.[183]

---

179. Of the members of the family identified by Lau, two of Dietrich's three sons were *scabini*: Ludwig and Dietrich. Two of Ludwig's four sons were *scabini*; of the other two, one was a *frater scabinorum* and the other a monk at the important abbey of St. Martin in Cologne. Three of the younger Dietrich's four sons were *scabini*; the fourth was a canon at St. Kunibert. In the fourth generation of the family there were two more *scabini*, both of whom were deposed in 1259 along with their father, grandfather, and two uncles.

180. Hoeniger, "Die älteste Urkunde," p.255. One of the properties in Brigida parish was a "halla cum duabus mensis que opposita est halle panificum inter caligatores." Cf. also H. II, p.320 (Scab. 2 XIV 3) in which Dietrich's widow wills two of the properties to her son Dietrich.

181. Gottfried was a parish official there (Hoeniger, "Die älteste Urkunde," p.255). Ludwig lived there, perhaps in his parents' house (Planitz and Buyken, *Schreinsbücher* 393).

182. Planitz and Buyken, *Schreinsbücher* 235; *Quellen* II 137. Full possession of a mill was significant property and represented a substantial income; most mills were owned by several people. Ludwig's son Heinrich received the mill and the debts owing to it as his share of his father's property: ... ita quod iure et sine contradictione ipsum molendinum cum debitis, que in panificibus reliquerint et panificibus absque domibus panificum obtinebit. Heinrich renounced his rights in all his father's other property. Ludwig's son Dietrich had valuable mercantile property among the cloth merchants: Planitz and Buyken, *Schreinsbücher* 1098.

183. H. II, p.201 (Nied. 13 III 15): Berwicus de Niederich et uxor sua Richmudis contradiderunt et remiserunt Richmudi filie eorum et Theoderico marito suo de Mulengazzen domum et aream que dicitur Widedure ... quam idem Theodericus et Richmudis uxor sua edificaverunt et in qua manent. ...

Aside from their milling interests, nothing is known of the occupation or business interests of the von Mühlengassen family. It is significant that, when they were banned from Cologne for the last time in 1268, most of the family went to other German cities, such as Neuss and Frankfurt.[184] The difficulties of the family, which led to some form of exile four times in forty-three years (1225–68), are part and parcel of Cologne history in the thirteenth century. After the banishment of 1268, the members of the family that had dominated the scabinal college and had almost controlled Cologne itself in the first half of the thirteenth century left Cologne for good to seek their fortunes elsewhere.

The Cleingedank (also *subtili mente* or *parvi mentes*) family is first recorded in Cologne in the last few decades of the twelfth century. The number of burghers who bore the name Cleingedank is great. When this is taken together with the widespread occurrence of the name in other western German towns (Strassburg, Siegburg, Mainz, Arnsberg) it may well suggest that we are dealing with more than one family. Nevertheless, the main lines of the prominent Cleingedank in Cologne are clear.[185] The first Cleingedank to appear in the records are Heinrich and Everhard. They may have been brothers; at least, some relation probably existed between them.[186] Heinrich Cleingedank was a member of

---

184. Von Winterfeld, *Handel, Kapital, und Patriziat*, p.37, who also presents some other circumstantial evidence for their mercantile activity; Lau, *Mitteilungen* 26, pp.126–9.

185. Lau, *Mitteilungen* 25, pp.370–4, reduces the chaos to two main lines and provides genealogical references. Von Winterfeld, *Handel, Kapital, und Patriziat*, p.31, points out the widespread occurrence of the same name and believes that this indicates some connection between the branches of one family although, as she indicates, this cannot be demonstrated.

186. Von Winterfeld, ibid., thinks they are brothers. A witness list of 1168 (H. II, p.296, n.5) lists them under the *cives*: Everardus, Apollonius, Heidenricus (=Heinrich, Henricus?) Cleingedank. Von Winterfeld's conjecture may well be correct; the first three witnesses listed under the *cives* are grouped together as the sons of Hartmann, the next three may be grouped together as Cleingedank. Apollonius is a common name in the Cleingedank family and not at all common in other families. Some weight is added to this possible connection by an entry in the registry of the *scabini* from ca.1197–1212 (H. II, p.304: Scab. 2 IV 10). Apollonius and Hermann, the sons of Heinrich Cleingedank, receive their inheritance from their father. A stipulation of the agreement is that one twenty-eighth of the house

the *Richerzeche* ca.1180.[187] No offices are recorded for Everhard, but the descendants of both men were *scabini*, town councilors, and members of the *Richerzeche* in the thirteenth and fourteenth centuries.

Heinrich Cleingedank lived in Alban parish; Everhard Cleingedank in Lawrence parish.[188] Each man acquired or inherited land in various parts of the city. Heinrich had property in Alban, Martin, Brigida, Niederich, and Gereon parishes. The property was diverse, ranging from market stalls and storehouses in Martin to agricultural land in Gereon.[189] Presumably these were fields planted in grain because in 1246 Gerhard and Appollonius Cleingedank (either the sons or the grandsons of Heinrich) arranged terms with the provost and chapter of St. Gereon to plant a vineyard in the fields they held from the church, fields which had formerly been planted with grain.[190] Everhard Cleingedank, in

---

Heinrich lives in is to be reserved for the children of Dietrich von Velthusin, who are still minors. But Dietrich is the son-in-law of Everhard Cleingedank, and Everhard guarantees the effestucation by the children by pledging one fourth of his house as security. Other explanations would be possible for this one-twenty-eighth interest the children of Dietrich have in Heinrich's *mansio*, but the simplest explanation is that Dietrich's wife, Everhard's daughter, had the interest in the house by heredity (note that the children, not Dietrich, have the interest). This, then, would seem to indicate some connection between the branch of the family headed by Everhard and the one headed by Heinrich.

187. Von Loesch I 13; Hoeniger, "Die älteste Urkunde," p.265, gives some references for him. Heinrich is never mentioned as a *scabinus*; in fact, in at least two instances, he appears among the *cives*, after the *scabini*: H. II, p.296, n.5 (1168); Korth, "Liber privilegiorum," p.203 (1184).

188. Hoeniger, "Die älteste Urkunde," p.265; H. I, p.248 (Laur. 4 II 7).

189. Hoeniger, "Die älteste Urkunde," p.265; H. II, p.304 (Scab. 2 IV 10). The property inherited by Heinrich's sons consists of four houses and a bake-house but H. II, pp.304–5 (Scab. 2 V 1) relating the inheritance of another son Philip includes a large number of *cellarii* and *cubiculi* as well as two *areas* in Gereon.

190. *Quellen* II 248. They had held twelve *iurnales* from the church for a tithe of the grain. This is to be converted into payment of one and one-half casks of wine of good quality, such as sold for 4 d. Cologne money. If the vineyard fails and they plant grain instead, the tithe is to be restored. There is no provision in the agreement we have for a period of no payment during which time the vines might grow. Gerhard and Appollonius acquired other land in Gereon as well: Planitz and Buyken, *Schreinsbücher* 430.

addition to his residence in Lawrence parish opposite the archbishop's palace, had property in Martin, Niederich, and Gereon parishes. He too had market stalls in Martin and land in Gereon. Probably the most significant property he held, aside from his residence, was the *curia* of Almer the *Vogt*, which he held in fief from the von Volmutstein family, a leading family of *ministeriales*.[191]

Many of the Cleingedank were active participants in the patrician wars. In 1259, for example, five of the twenty-five burghers who were exiled by the archbishop and his party were members of the Cleingedank family.[192] There is no direct evidence of mercantile activity by the Cleingedank—and no direct evidence of connection to the *ministeriales*. A Bruno Cleingedank is mentioned as a *miles* in 1216 and a Richwin Cleingedank as a *miles* later in the thirteenth century, but no connection can be shown between these men and the bourgeois Cleingedank.[193] The bourgeois family remained important in Cologne well into the fourteenth century.

Waldever was a subadvocate of Cologne in the thirteenth century (he was dead by 1263) and an important member of the Overstolz faction, of which his father-in-law Gottschalk Overstolz was the head, during the patrician wars. Waldever's family never adopted a lasting name in this period, but it can be followed back into the 1170's to a certain Otto and his wife Odierna, who were both dead at that time.[194] The son of Otto and Odierna, Waldever, was the first of the family to achieve prominence; he was a member of the *Richerzeche* and a *scabinus* in the 1170's and 1180's.[195] His son, called Waldever *super forum* or *de foro*, does not seem to have held any office; but his grandson was the Waldever the subadvocate mentioned above. Waldever the subadvocate's son, Heinrich de Ripa, continued the family tradition as subadvocate

---

191. Lawrence parish: H. I, p.248 (Laur. 4 II 7); pp.251–2 (Laur. 4 III 10); H. II, p.304 (Scab. 2 IV 11): domus opposite palacio archiepiscopi in qua mansit Everardus Kleynegedanc. Martin parish: H. I, p.95 (Mart. 6 II 16): Everhard lent money on a *taberna* and *mensa* in the cloth merchants' quarter. The *curia Almeri advocati* is also in Martin: H. II, p.304 (Scab. 2 IV 9), p.322 (Scab. 2 XV 7). Gereon parish: H. II, p.224 (Ger. 2 I 1). Niederich parish: H. II, p.149 (Nied. 10 IX 6).

192. Lau, *Mitteilungen* 25, p.370. Lacomblet II 467.

193. Von Winterfeld, *Handel, Kapital, und Patriziat*, p.31.

194. Lau, *Mitteilungen* 24, pp.88–9, provides genealogical information.

195. Ibid., p.89; Hoeniger, "Die älteste Urkunde," pp.258–9.

and a member of the *Richerzeche* near the end of the thirteenth century.[196]

Waldever, the son of Otto and Odierna, owned a large business house in the market area. This was inherited by his son Waldever *super forum*, who added to it a substantial holding in Severin parish.[197] After Heinrich de Ripa, who was dead by 1314, the family seems to have ended in female descendants and males without heirs.[198]

Four families, whose members did not hold office until the early thirteenth century (the Overstolz, Gir, Hardevust, and Birkelin families) and one prominent burgher (Dietrich von der Ehrenpforte) complete our survey of the patriciate from about 1150 to about 1230.

The Overstolz family led the victorious faction in the patrician wars of the thirteenth century. The first member of the family to appear in the town records is Gottschalk Overstolz, who lived in Airsbach (he is sometimes called "de Oversburg"). Gottschalk's will is included in the town records. He left to his heirs twelve entire houses, other parts of houses coming to a total of about two and two-thirds additional houses, two shops (*cubiculi*), and one and one-half sales stalls (*mensae*), and numerous cellars (*cellaria*). This does not include his mobile wealth, which must have been substantial. Most of the residential property was located in Airsbach, most of the market property in Martin and Brigida parishes.[199]

Gottschalk's sons acquired rural land and more extensive holdings in the town. His eldest son Gunter, who was already dead at the time of his father's will, had eight *iurnales* of land just outside the walls of Cologne.[200] Another son, Richolf, acquired extensive holdings in the village of Hurth, including forest, fields, and a mill, land that previously belonged to the archbishop's butler.[201] A third son, Gottschalk,

196. Lau, *Mitteilungen* 24, pp.88–9.

197. Hoeniger, "Die älteste Urkunde," pp.258–9.

198. Lau, admittedly only going to 1325, lists only one male descendant of Waldever the *Vogt* who might have had heirs in the fourteenth century. The other lines of the family (descended from Waldever's brothers) seem never to have achieved great importance.

199. Lau, *Mitteilungen* 24, pp.71–80, provides genealogical information. H. II, pp.318–9 (Scab. 2 XIII 1–9). His residence in Airsbach is described as "domus cum curte mansio"; thus it may have been substantial.

200. *Quellen* II 1.

201. *Quellen* II 148 (1234): Richolf's will. The property is described as

acquired an urban *Hof*, the Cederwald.[202] And a fourth son, Heinrich, received some chambers next to the mint in Cologne from the archbishop as an hereditary fief. They had previously been held on a similar basis by the von der Ehrenpforte family.[203]

The first member of the family to hold office was the younger Gottschalk, who is mentioned as a *scabinus* in the 1230's.[204] A Johann Overstolz, who cannot be established in the genealogy of the family, was also a *scabinus* in the same period.[205] From this time on, the Overstolz were represented in all areas of political life.

The Overstolz family is the only major patrician family that without any doubt had a mercantile background. Gottschalk the elder owned and worked in a shop in the drapers' quarter (*inter watmengeros*) of Martin parish.[206] Thus a definite connection between this prominent family and an important sector of Cologne commerce, the textile trade, can be shown.

The first mention of a man with the name Birkelin in town records occurs already in the middle of the twelfth century with Hermann Birkelin and his son Gerhard; however, the first Birkelin whose relationship to the later members of the family can be shown is Werner Birkelin, whom the abbot of Erbach called a "noble citizen of Cologne" in 1215, sometime after Werner's death.[207] Hermann Birkelin lived in Lawrence parish, but Werner lived in Brigida and held a little property in Martin as well.[208] Werner's son, also named Hermann, left a testament which provided that six and three-fourths houses (of which

---

"predium in silvis et agris . . . molendinum cum pratis, prout in villa predicta et circa continentur" and as lands "que fuerunt pincerne."

202. *Quellen* II 140, 141 (1233).

203. *Quellen* II 174 (1238): cameras prope monetam Coloniensem sitas ipsi (Henrico) et suis heredibus tam masculis quam feminis concessimus perpetuo a nobis et successoribus nostris in feodo tenendas.

204. *Quellen* II 166 (1237).

205. Lau, *Mitteilungen* 24, pp.71–2.

206. H. I, p.214 (Mart. 20 VI 4). The key words are "in quo olim stetit Godescalcus Overstolz."

207. H. I, p. 223 (Laur. 2 I 5: ca.1135–65). *Quellen* II 49 (1215). Lau, *Mitteilungen* 25, pp.363–7, provides genealogical information.

208. H. I, p.223 (Laur. 2 I 5): hanc domum havin gemachet, da si inne wonahtich sint. Lau, *Mitteilungen* 25, p.363; von Winterfeld, *Handel, Kapital, und Patriziat* p.38; H. I, p.155 (Mart. 10 IV 12).

four were probably quite small) and a bakehouse be divided up among six heirs.[209] The amount of property is not very impressive.

Werner Birkelin is not recorded as having held office, but his son Hermann was a *scabinus* by 1218 and his sons Gerhard and Werner were *fratres scabinorum* by 1230.[210] Later the family was represented among the *scabini*, in the *Richerzeche*, and on the town council; but, with the exception of one more *frater scabinorum*, this activity cannot be documented until the first decades of the fourteenth century.[211]

The family may have been involved in commerce at the end of the twelfth century, but there is no direct evidence for this. Their wide-ranging contacts with Erbach, Mainz, and Liége as well as their market property could indicate some mercantile activity. Many of the Birkelin left the bourgeoisie, but the family maintained its position in Cologne at least until the end of the fourteenth century.[212]

Albero Hardevust appears in the twelfth-century gild list of St. Martin, along with a relative Fortlief Hardevust, and in the earliest parish records of St. Martin.[213] Albero is called *dominus* in the records, but he apparently did not hold any office;[214] in one document he is even clearly separated from the parish magistrates of St. Martin.[215] The first members of the family to have offices were Hildiger and Heinrich

---

209. *Quellen* II 131 (1232).

210. *Quellen* II 59 (1218); Lau, *Mitteilungen* 25, p.364.

211. Ibid.

212. Von Winterfeld, *Handel, Kapital, und Patriziat*, p.38, states, regarding the inheritance left by Hermann Birkelin: "Man erkennt sofort, dass dieser Nachlass nur einem Kaufmann gehören konnte." She makes this statement, apparently, because the property is partially mercantile and in parts of houses. She goes on to note that some members of one line of the family (the Birkelin vom Horne) were engaged in the wine trade in the fourteenth century and, with this as a basis, sees the Birkelin as wine merchants earlier as well because of their ties to the abbey of Erbach, the Church of St. Stephen in Mainz, and to the bishop of Liège. This may constitute the basis for a guess, but not for proof.

213. H. II, pt.2, pp.16, 19. H. I, pp.15–16 (Mart. 1 II 10). Lau provides full genealogical references: *Mitteilungen* 26, pp.104–9. That Albero and Fortlif were related is indicated by H. I, p.24 (Mart. 2 I 17) where reference is made to "Herimannum consanguinem Alberonis Hardevust et Fortlivi."

214. H. I, p.108 (Mart. 7 II 27).

215. H. I, p.25 (Mart. 2 I 20).

Hardevust, grandsons of Albero, who were *fratres scabinorum* in 1230. Only three members of the family were *scabini* before 1325, but in the *Richerzeche* and on the town council they were somewhat more important.[216]

Albero's property lay primarily in Martin parish. He apparently purchased the house in the Rheingasse, in which he lived.[217] Most of the major residences of the Hardevust remained in Martin parish although one branch of the family acquired a *curia* in the Friesenstrasse near St. Gereon at the end of the thirteenth century.[218] Other properties held by family members were located in many areas of the city by the middle of the thirteenth century, including a vineyard and the unusual total of four mills on the river.[219]

The occupation of the early Hardevust is not known. They had sufficient mobile wealth, like almost all the great families, to make loans. One member of a collateral branch of the family is listed as a member of the gild *unter den Gaddemen*, the gild of cloth merchants, and one is listed as a goldsmith in 1325.[220]

The name Gir or *avarus* is another example of a nickname like Jude or Cleingedank. It was also the basis of a pun when Gir was occasionally transformed into Geyer (vulture). The first member of the Gir family of which we have knowledge is Hartmann Gir, the son of a certain Heinrich.[221] Hartmann's sons Dietrich and Gerhard were *scabini* in the

---

216. Lau, *Mitteilungen* 26, p.104.

217. H. I, p.31 (Mart. 2 II 4). It may be significant that Albero and his wife purchased the house "de propria pecunia." Some have interpreted this to mean that the patriciate was defined in Cologne as a group of *viri hereditarii*, similar to those in Ghent (von Winterfeld, *Handel, Kapital, und Patriziat*, p.5). In this line of interpretation, the insistence that Albero bought the house with his own money indicates that he was acquiring an *hereditas* and thus, in effect, joining the patriciate. As far as I can see, the chief force of the argument is the analogy to Ghent. Aside from the phrase "de propria pecunia," no direct "evidence" of a group of *viri hereditarii* exists in Cologne.

218. Lau, *Mitteilungen* 26, p.104.

219. *Quellen* II 297 (1251); von Winterfeld, *Handel, Kapital, und Patriziat*, p.49.

220. Lau, *Mitteilungen* 26, p.105; von Winterfeld, *Handel, Kapital, und Patriziat*, p.49, states that Bruno Hardevust was a merchant in England in 1224; she does not indicate her evidence.

221. Lau, *Mitteilungen* 25, pp.375–7, provides genealogical information.

1230's and were deposed and exiled in 1259. Most of the prominent members of the Gir family were descended from Gerhard. This branch provided several *scabini, Bürgermeister, Rentenmeister*, and members of the *Richerzeche* and the town council in the thirteenth and fourteenth centuries.[222]

Hartmann Gir resided in Martin parish, and he acquired numerous properties throughout Cologne, especially in Martin and Airsbach parishes. In addition to various houses, he possessed several mercantile *cubiculi* and a vineyard near the church of St. Kunibert.[223] Hartmann's son Dietrich acquired two important properties (*curiae*), Covoltzhof and Gürzenich, in Alban parish, which had previously belonged to landed lords and which were, with their orchards, fields, and turrets, the closest thing to manor houses inside Cologne.[224]

Although concrete evidence is lacking, the Gir family seems to be an example of a mercantile family that accumulated sufficient wealth to enter the patriciate in the thirteenth century. Reference is made to the *cubiculum* of Hartmann Gir in Cologne records.[225] Since the reference is incidental, it may indicate that the *cubiculum* was a shop in which Hartmann worked and not just mercantile property which he owned; however, this is by no means certain in the way that a reference to a "cubiculum in quo Hartmannus stat" would be. The pattern of land

---

222. Ibid.; Lacomblet II 465, 467.

223. No full testament for Hartman exists in the Cologne records, but the inheritance of his daughter Gertrude and her husband Simon the viscount—five houses, one third of another house and one fourth of another, one and one-half *cubiculi*, and a vineyard—indicates Hartmann's substantial wealth. Cf. *Quellen* II 219. There were three other heirs, and Hartmann made bequests for himself and his wife such as the house he left to the Benedictines (*Quellen* II 128). Dietrich's share of the inheritance is included, along with the dowry Dietrich's wife brought him, in Planitz and Buyken, *Schreinsbücher* 710.

I know of no proof to substantiate the claim of von Winterfeld, *Handel, Kapital, und Patriziat*, p.42, that Hartmann inherited no real property at all; but where it is possible to trace his property, he did purchase it or receive it on default of a debt. Cf., for example, Planitz and Buyken, *Schreinsbücher* 696; H. II, p.319 (Scab. 2 XIII 10).

224. Covoltzhof acquired from the Count of Arberg and his family: H. II, p.295, n.7, and *Quellen* II 129 (shortly after 1232). Gürzenich acquired from Arnold von Vrechen and others: *Quellen* II 147 (1234).

225. *Quellen* II 106 (1227); similar evidence exists for his son Dietrich: Planitz and Buyken, *Schreinsbücher* 566.

acquisition in the early thirteenth century provides additional circumstantial evidence that the Gir family had recently acquired wealth. They invested first in rents and loans secured by urban property and then in prestige properties like Covoltzhof and Gürzenich. In a society like that of medieval Cologne, this accumulation of wealth and property would have paved the way for membership in the patriciate. The Gir family remained prominent in urban affairs into the fourteenth century.

In addition to these families, one outstanding individual of the early thirteenth century must be mentioned, Dietrich von der Ehrenpforte, one of the few patricians for whom there is a literary source. During the contest between Philip of Swabia and Otto of Brunswick for the leadership of Germany, the archbishop and the town favored Otto. Caesarius of Heisterbach, in one of his little moral tracts, describes Dietrich as a leading citizen of the town who deserted Otto and let Philip into the town; Caesarius hints at bribery.[226] Confirmation of Dietrich's support of Philip is given in Philip's grant of protection to the convent of Weiher. Philip takes the convent under his protection "for the sake of the soul of our servant (*fidelis*) of blessed memory, Dietrich de Erinporze, who is buried there."[227] Dietrich's privileges in the toll and the mint had also been excepted from Philip's decision to liquidate them in 1207.[228]

Dietrich was a *scabinus* and held certain properties near the Cologne mint from the archbishop in feudal tenure (*in feodo tenebant*). His father Dietrich and his son Hildeger held the property before and after him in a similar fashion.[229] Although feudal tenure was not common for a citizen of the town, it was not unknown. The burger Werner de Monticulo gave the church of St. Ursula all his land, both that held

---

226. Caesarius of Heisterbach, *Dialogus Miraculorum*, ed. Josef Strange (Köln-Bonn-Brussels, 1851) 6. 27., pp.379–80.

227. Lacomblet II 20: . . . suscipimus defensionem, et pro remedio anime fidelis nostri beate memorie Diderici de Erinporze, qui ibidem sepultus est. . . . .

228. Philip of Swabia, "Pactum cum Coloniensibus," *MGH. LL.* Sect. IV, pt.2, pp.14–15: Item cuicumque civium Adolfus archiepiscopus quondam vel Bruno archiepiscopus monete vel telonei reditus impignoraverint, ipsi debitum suum recipient, et nichil preter sortem, exceptis feodis et Theoderico de Erenporzen, qui optinebit pignora et beneficia in moneta secundum privilegium ab Adolfo archiepiscopo sibi collatum.

229. *Quellen* II 174. Dietrich was also an archiepiscopal *ministerialis* in the period 1218–38; cf. Pötter, p.38.

OFFICES BEFORE 1230

A. Did not form *Geschlecht*: twelfth century

	family	ministeriales	merchants	scabini	Richerzeche	thelonearii	subadvocate, viscount	land in villages	parish of residence
1.	Ungemaz	X				X	X	X	Lawrence
2.	Minnevuz	X	*				X	X	Martin
3.	von Salzgassen	X		X	X	X			Alban
4.	de Hoie		*	X	X				Martin, Airsbach
5.	de s. Laurentio					X			Lawrence
6.	de Macellis	X		X					Martin
7.	Wolbero, filius Sigewini	X		X			X		Martin
8.	Suevus			X					Martin
9.	Canus			X				X	Lawrence
10.	Niger			X				X	Lawrence, Martin
11.	de s. Cecilia			X				X	
12.	Saphir						X	X	Martin
13.	de s. Albano			X	X			X	Alban
14.	Flacco			X	X			X	Alban

B. Formed *Geschlecht*: twelfth century

#	Family											Churches
15.	Jude	X	*	X	X	X	X	X	X	X	X	Martin
16.	Raitze	X		X	X	X	X	X	X		X	Martin
17.	von Mummersloch	X	*	X	X	X	X	X	X		X	Alban
18.	Grin			X	X	X	X	X				Niederich
19.	Scherfgin			X	X	X	X	X	X			Martin
20.	Parfuse	X	*	X	X	X	X	X	X			Brigida, Columba
21.	von Muhlengassen			X	X	X	X	X	X			Brigida, Holy Apostles, Niederich
22.	Cleingedank			X	X	X	X	X				Alban, Lawrence
23.	Waldever the Vogt			X	X	X	X	X	X			Martin

C. Did not form *Geschlecht*: early thirteenth century

#	Family											Churches
24.	von der Ehrenpforte			X						X		Lawrence

D. Formed *Geschlecht*: early thirteenth century

#	Family											Churches
25.	Overstolz	X									X	Airsbach
26.	Birkelin		*							X		Brigida
27.	Hardevust	X								X		Martin
28.	Gir		*									Martin

Summary table. Families are listed in this table in the order in which they are discussed in the text. Twelfth-century individuals known to us only as *scabini* have not been included.

Determining the ministerial or mercantile status of a family is the most difficult task. For mercantile status two symbols are used: "*" indicates some cause to believe the family was mercantile; an "X" indicates that the family was, in all probability, mercantile.

feudally and that held for a rent, in 1176.[230] This probably refers to lands held by feudal tenure near Cologne, both inside and outside the walls. In Dietrich's case, however, it is possible that the fiefs held from the archbishop were fiefs pertaining to the mint, that is *Hausgenossenschaft* fiefs. Dietrich did not establish a patrician *Geschlecht*.

The evidence for Cologne in the twelfth century presents a bourgeois style of life common to most patricians. The dominant characteristic that appears in the sources is the diversity of their investments. A typical patrician family had investments in urban and rural land, in rents, in moneylending, and, probably, in commerce.

The primary purpose of the town records was to register land transactions; consequently, evidence for the possession of land is the best evidence we have. Landholding was not confined to urban properties; many patricians either inherited or invested in rural lands, primarily in villages in the immediate vicinity of Cologne. One bit of evidence suggests that investment in rural land was common early in the history of Cologne. Walgerus, a man of great wealth who lived in the city, is recorded in 1022 as holding land outside the city in the village of Rodenkirchen, for which he owed the *villicus* of Rodenkirchen a measure of oats. The words used to describe Walgerus make it probable that he was an early merchant who invested in rural land. The evidence for Walgerus is more than a century older than that for any other burgher.[231]

By the latter half of the twelfth century it was fairly common for a patrician to possess rural land. The land could be held on a variety of tenures and for a variety of purposes. Some land inside the city, especially in the outlying parishes, and land just outside the walls of 1180 was put to agricultural use. The large holdings (*curiae* or *Höfe*) will be discussed later, but patricians also had smaller holdings, such as the twelve *iurnales* of grain fields that the Cleingedank brothers converted into vineyard around 1234. Documented holdings outside the city or its immediate vicinity are almost all in villages very near Cologne,

---

230. Lacomblet I 461.

231. *Quellen* I 21. Walgerus is described as "vir quidam opibus predives vocabulo Walgerus." Clearly the person who drafted the document regarded his wealth as more important than his social standing. Walgerus held the land in Rodenkirchen but lived in Cologne: "platee que nuncupata Wizechini inhabitor fuit." It is impossible to determine whether Walgerus had the land originally and then moved to Cologne and became rich; or whether he became rich and then invested in the land. That he did the latter is speculation on my part.

such as Hönnigen, Pafferode, Gunthersdorp, Merheim, and Rodenkirchen. The only exception I have found to this is the vineyard at Remagen owned by Daniel and Bruno Jude. In the period 1160 to 1200, members of ten families held land in villages near Cologne (see the accompanying table). In most cases it cannot be determined exactly how the land was obtained, but the example of the holdings of the de s. Cecilia and the Raitze at Hönnigen is suggestive. Albero de s. Cecilia lent 69m. to Karl of Hönnigen; the security on the loan was the usufruct in substantial property in Hönnigen. Later, Heinrich Raitze inherited by way of his mother, the niece of Albero de s. Cecilia, a *curia* in Hönnigen. It may well be that this land, and more like it, came into the hands of burghers as a result of default on a debt. Other land was purchased (such as the fifteen *iurnales* that Heinrich Flacco acquired at Geine) and still other land was held from a church (such as the holdings of the Jude at Dünwald). Thus there is direct evidence that rural land was acquired through debt, purchase, and the acceptance of a benefice; there is no direct evidence that any of these men migrated from these villages, where they retained some landed interests, to Cologne although this must remain a possibility.

The majority of the property held by patricians was in Cologne itself. It consisted of residences, market property, agricultural land in the outlying areas, and such structures as mills. Unless the property was used by the owner himself, it was used as security for loans or let out on an annual rent. Urban property and rents derived from it were an important part of a patrician's fortune. A typical patrician had a mixture of residential and market property (of course, sometimes the property served both functions). It could be divided into the smallest fractions and acquired through inheritance or purchase. Generally the property was scattered throughout the city or at least throughout a parish. Since the property that a patrician inherited was usually scattered and in fractions, there was a natural tendency towards consolidation.

The acquisition of extensive properties occurred in one of two ways. Either one heir of a wealthy patrician attempted to reconsolidate his father's holdings in a given area, adding to it what he could of his neighbors' property; or a large estate in the city was purchased or held from a nonresident owner. Since opportunities for consolidation and for the acquisition of large estates were much fewer in Martin parish, this process occurred mostly in the sparsely populated areas of the old city (especially Alban parish) and in the outlying areas (such as Gereon, Airsbach, Severin parishes). In this way families that had made their fortune in trade and quite possibly were still engaged in trade could leave the ancestral house on the market and participate in a medieval equivalent of a "flight to the suburbs."[232] The Parfuse are an example of a family that moved from Brigida to Alban parish. The Berlicher Hof, in which Richolf Parfuse the Younger lived, was consolidated on the basis of a property acquired by his father, who still lived in his property on the Mühlengasse in Brigida parish. By the time Richolf the Younger was done, Berlich included orchards, vineyards, and an old Roman tower. Apparently, in the first part of the thirteenth century, patrician families felt they should live in more splendor than a house on the market could afford.

The easier way to acquire a compact holding was to receive it or acquire it from a nonresident owner. Thus Karl the *thelonearius* and his daughter held Covoltzhof in hereditary tenure from the *Burggraf* in the 1180's, and Dietrich Gir bought the urban estate from the von Arsberg family around 1232. Dietrich Gir, in fact, held two prestige properties, the Covoltzhof and the Gürzenicher Hof. In most cases these urban estates had been acquired, either as a whole or piece by piece. There is little evidence, if any, to support the idea that landed proprietors in Cologne holding large blocks of urban land, profited simply from rising rents. The only ones who actually held such tracts of land were families, like that of the von Arsberg, or ecclesiastical foundations, like St. Gereon. Rents were an important source of income to the patriciate, but they were not mere windfalls for the lucky men who happened to own land in or near the expanding town. There is no evidence that suggests that the patriciate had been a *rentier* group from the beginning.[233]

After the possession of real property, the next most likely income to appear in the records is the income from moneylending. By the thirteenth century it had become so important that special books were established by the parishes for these records. With a few exceptions, the sums lent in the twelfth century do not seem to have been very large. The most notable exceptions are the amounts lent by Gerhard Ungemaz, including the 600m. he lent the archbishop. Those who borrowed were customarily burghers, patrician and nonpatrician alike, and only occa-

---

232. Ironically, one of the "suburbs" was the underpopulated parish of St. Alban within the old Roman walls. Von Winterfeld, *Handel, Kapital, und Patriziat*, p.16, discusses Alban as a medieval "suburb."

233. Von Winterfeld, ibid., pp.66–7, argues this convincingly. She points out, first, that large blocks of land were not in the hands of burghers in the earliest period; second, that the *Erbleihe* (an hereditary lease with a fixed annual rent) was used much more often than a short-term lease with a negotiable rent.

sionally a rural figure like Karl von Hönnigen, who borrowed the 69m. from Albero de s. Cecilia.

It is hard to imagine that the economic growth responsible for the development of Cologne had no effect on the civic leaders of the new town. Unfortunately, direct evidence of commercial activity on the part of the political elite in Cologne is meager; but circumstantial evidence makes it probable that certain members of the patriciate took part in the commercial life of the city (see the accompanying table). None of the leading men is designated directly as a merchant or can be shown to have been active in the English trade, the Flemish trade, or any of the traditional areas of Cologne commerce. The one bit of firm evidence for mercantile activity is a reference in the town records to a given *cubiculum* in which a certain person "stands" or "stood." Since the merchant frequently retailed his wares, this is good evidence of mercantile occupation. Two of the men discussed above were merchants by this criterion: Emund de Macellis and Gottschalk Overstolz, the "founder" of that prestigious family. The men who used other *cubiculi* and *mensae* are often identified in the records, but they were not patricians.

Other indicators of mercantile occupation must be used with care. If a man is listed on the twelfth-century gild list of St. Martin, it is highly likely he was a merchant although the members of the merchant gild are difficult to distinguish from the citizens of the parish community on the list.[234] More doubtful evidence is the holding of property in the market area. Many people had property in the market area who were clearly not merchants. Mere possession of market property may help to create the impression a man was a merchant, but it is not sufficient to prove that he was one. Evidence that members of a patrician family were merchants in later centuries does not lead necessarily to the conclusion that their ancestors were merchants too. But here, as with market property, circumstantial evidence may provide certain clues.

By these criteria other families were, in all probability, involved in business. Albero Hardevust appears on the twelfth-century citizen and gild list of St. Martin. If the fact that some Hardevust can be proved to have been merchants in the fourteenth century and the fact that the Hardevust held market property are added to this, it must appear quite probable that the family had commercial interests from the twelfth

234. Von Loesch, *Die Kölner Kaufmannsgilde*, pp.13–20, interprets the entries on the list. Most of the new members listed in the period 1130–80 are added to two columns, indicating that they became members of the merchant gild and the parish organization at the same time.

century on. The Scherfgin follow the same pattern with the exception that the Scherfgin on the citizen and gild list cannot be identified in the genealogy of the family. A third case of town leaders who were probably merchants is Sigewin the viscount and his son Wolbero. Naturally their heirs cannot be shown to have been merchants, but both are listed more than once on the citizens and gild list, and their property lay in the market area.

After the Overstolz and Emund de Macellis and after the Hardevust, the Scherfgin, and Sigewin *comes*, the next families which were most likely to have been mercantile are the Minnevuz, Parfuse, de Hoie, Suevus, Jude, von Mummersloch, Birkelin, and Gir. As in most cases, market property can be shown for all these families; in addition, each has some small indication that sets it apart from the families that merely had market property. The de Hoie and the Suevus have names that indicate an origin, respectively, in Huy and Swabia. The Minnevuz and the Parfuse were descended from Rainer of Basel, who quite probably had come to Cologne recently since the property inherited by his children came mostly from their mother. Admittedly, this evidence on the basis of names is weak, but it does distinguish this group somewhat from those who simply had market property.[235] Daniel and Bruno Jude had a vineyard in Remagen; this may well be an indication that they were involved in the lucrative wine trade. Hermann von Mummersloch helped settle a conflict between the Count of Altena and the burghers of Bremen around 1200; this, together with a draper named von Mummersloch documented for the fouteenth century, may indicate that the von Mummersloch family was engaged in commerce in the twelfth century. Some of the Birkelin family were engaged in the wine trade in the fourteenth century; perhaps other members of the family were merchants earlier. Finally, the Gir may have been merchants; the pattern of property acquisition, the *cubiculum* of Hartmann Gir, even the name itself may be small indications of this.

Quite clearly it is impossible to say whether the families in this third group were mercantile. Mercantile occupation is an even more difficult conclusion to make for those families whose sole claim to that title (in the records) is the possession of market property. Of those we have discussed, these families would be the von Mühlengassen, the Cleinge-dank, and the family of Waldever the *Vogt*. Another interesting, but doubtful case is the Grin family. There were merchants named Grin in

---

235. Some have even tried to use evidence from names to a ridiculous extreme. Thus Parfuse (=*Barfüsse* or *nudi pedes*) is supposed to have some connection to Piedpowder in reference to "dusty-footed" merchants.

the fourteenth century, but in the twelfth century the Grin were resident in Niederich for the most part and did not even own market land.

Finally are those families or individuals who held no market property and for whom other circumstantial evidence is lacking. The only patrician family that held power into the thirteenth century to be listed here would be the Raitze. But it includes all of the twelfth-century figures mentioned above, with the exception of Emund de Macellis, Sigewin the viscount and his son Wolbero, and the Minnevuz, de Hoie, and Suevus families. Especially in the case of the isolated twelfth-century figures, the lack of evidence must account for some of this. At the least these men may have held market property even though none can be documented for them. With few exceptions, then, it is only probable rather than certain that early patricians in Cologne were merchants. Sources of income and occupation are difficult questions to answer, and it is impossible even to estimate how large a proportion of patrician income derived from commerce.

The question of family origins is almost as difficult. Basically, our knowledge of patrician families only extends back to about 1150;[236] only two families (the Jude and the Raitze) can be traced back unmistakably into the first half of the twelfth century. By this time they were well established in an urban context. The two major hypotheses on the origins of the patriciate emphasize respectively

---

236. One major reason the families cannot be traced back into the early twelfth century with any confidence is the lack of family names in that period. The patricians gradually adopted family names in the course of the twelfth and thirteenth centuries, but it was a long time before such names were used with regularity. Some names cause little trouble; names such as Jude, Cleingedank, Gir, are distinctive enough and used with enough regularity to establish accurate information from the latter half of the twelfth century on. Other "names" (Albus, Niger, Suevus, etc.) are too general and are applied to too many people to be very useful. To complicate matters even more, many people changed their names. The most common change occurred with a change of residence. For example, Franco Birkelin became Franco de Cornu (vom Horne) because he resided in a house called *Ad Cornum*. The practice was common and can sometimes give an illusion of family continuity that did not exist. Another change might be the use of a mother's name rather than a father's name. It is for this reason that one branch of the Overstolz family is called Quattermart (Lau, *Mitteilungen* 24, p.80). Thus evidence derived from names alone can be very misleading. Unfortunately, for the period before 1150, even this misleading information is lacking.

long-distance traders (Pirenne, Planitz) and *ministeriales* (Hibbert, Les-tocquoy, Schulz).[237] But these two categories may not be mutually exclusive. Unless one assumes that all Cologne merchants were de-scended from rootless wanderers of an earlier period, there is no reason why they might not have been *ministeriales*. In fact there are too many examples in twelfth-century Cologne of men who were both burghers and *ministeriales* to deny the influence of *ministeriales* on urban life. It seems reasonable that they also may have engaged in trade even if direct

237. There are two major theses on the origins of merchants and the rise of the urban patriciate. In a number of works, Henri Pirenne put forth the thesis that the early merchants were "new men," men who had no ties to the previous economic system based on land. The patriciate which emerged was in turn founded by the descendants of these early drifters, provided the descendants were able to maintain the shrewdness and the ability of their ancestors. Pirenne put the matter clearly in "The Stages in the Social History of Capitalism," *AHR* 19 (1913–14), p.502: "The ancestors of the bourgeoisie must then be sought, specifically, in the mass of those wandering beings who, having no land to cultivate, floated across the surface of society, living from day to day upon the alms of monasteries, hiring themselves to the cultivators of the soil in harvest time, enlisting in the armies in time of war, and shrinking from neither pillage nor rapine if the occasion presented itself. It may without difficulty be admitted that there may have been among them some rural artisans or professional peddlers. But it is beyond question that with very few exceptions it was poor men who floated to the towns and there built up the first fortunes in movable property that the Middle Ages knew."

Another thesis, more recently espoused by Jacques Lestocquoy, *Les Villes de Flandre et d'Italie sous le gouvernement des patriciens* (XIe-XVe siècle) (Paris, 1952) and by A. B. Hibbert, "The Origins of the Medieval Town Patriciate," *Past and Present*, no.3 (Feb. 1953), pp.15–27, places a major emphasis on free landed proprietors and, especially, on *ministeriales* as important sources for the mercantile group and for the urban patriciate.

The question has been argued in Lucien Febvre, Jean Lestocquoy, and Georges Espinas, "Fils de riches ou nouveaux riches," *AESC* I (1946), pp.139–53.

Certainly the evidence from Cologne sheds no light on the question of the origins of merchants. It does not go very far, either, in clarifying the origins of the patriciate. As Lestocquoy himself notes (*AESC* I, p.146) the genealogies begin too late in Cologne. But certain points made by Lestocquoy must be admitted on the basis of the evidence from Cologne. First, the Church was not so hostile to the new commerce that it was not quite possible to be a dependent of one church or the other and a merchant. Second, one could be both a *ministerialis* and a burgher. Third, the patriciate in Cologne arose from several groups; and its most distinctive

evidence of commercial activity is lacking for them, as it is for almost all burghers.

The *burgenses* (the term is used in Cologne for the first time in 1143)[238] were a new group in medieval society in the twelfth century. They undoubtedly arose from several groups; however, there is no evidence that the patricians derived from powerful groups in landed society. The extensive estates inside and outside the town held by certain patrician families in the thirteenth and fourteenth centuries had been acquired, usually through purchase. No nobles or men of similar standing lived in Cologne in the twelfth century, except, of course, the archbishop. The greater families of the rank of *ministeriales*, who form a distinct group in the documents of the twelfth century, did not live in Cologne for the most part nor did they participate in urban affairs. They were on their way to becoming landed lords, what German authors call the *Landadel*, or local nobility, in distinction to the *Grossadel*, or high nobility. There can be no doubt that, whatever their origins, the patrician families began in relatively humble circumstances.[239]

With one outstanding exception (Richolf of Aachen), the influential *ministeriales* in Cologne were men who belonged to the lower ranks of

institution, the *Richerzeche*, represents an alliance between the mercantile leadership of Martin parish and the other families established in the old city and the other suburbs.

Remembering especially the role of the *ministeriales* in Cologne, we can agree with Jean Schneider, *La Ville de Metz aux XIIIe et XIVe siècles* (Nancy, 1950), p.65: ". . . les origines de patriciat posaient des problèmes; des travaux récents il se dégage déjà une conclusion: on ne peut assigner au patriciat une origine unique; il est issu de classes diverses. Ces questions se posent du reste dans des termes fort différents, selon qu'il s'agit des cités épiscopales anciennes ou des villes post-normandes." The assumption here is that in the old episcopal cities more established, nonmercantile groups played a larger role in the evolution of town life and institutions. This is borne out by the evidence from Cologne.

238. Maschke, "Continuité urbaine," p.938.

239. The following material on the *ministeriales* is based primarily on Jakob Ahrens, *Die Ministerialität in Köln und am Niederrhein* (Leipzig, 1908). Also useful is François-Louis Ganshof, *Etude sur les ministeriales en Flandre et en Lotharingie* (Brussels, 1926).

Friedrich Lau, *Die erzbischöflichen Beamten in der Stadt Köln während des zwölften Jahrhunderts* (Lübeck, 1891) provides information on the higher *ministeriales*. Several families had property in the town although they did not live there (cf. Hermann Keussen, *Topographie der Stadt Köln im Mittelalter* (Bonn, 1910) under Lawrence parish). The only high

the *ministeriales* of the archbishop, especially those who had the *ministerium* of a toll, or to the group of dependents of one of the local ecclesiastical foundations, such as the abbey of St. Martin. In the twelfth century the archbishop's *ministeriales* developed into two major groups. The higher *ministeriales* were those who held the offices of the court, offices such as marshal, chamberlain, and the like; they built up rural estates for their families and eventually joined the ranks of the local nobility. By the middle of the thirteenth century most of these men are designated in the charters not as *ministeriales* but as *milites*. It is to this group that the mid-twelfth century *Dienstrecht* of the Cologne *ministeriales* primarily applies.[240] The lower *ministeriales* had local offices, such as *Schultheiss* in a village of the archbishop or the office of toll collector. By the twelfth century those of this lower group who were resident in the town were indistinguishable from the other burghers. Their *ministeria* (tolls, the mint, etc.) were intimately involved in urban affairs, and they passed naturally from the ranks of the archbishop's dependents to positions of leadership in the town.

It was quite possible to be both a burgher and a *ministerialis*.[241] The twelfth century represents a very important transitional stage in the evolution of the *ministeriales*; it is not surprising that the same man will sometimes appear as a *ministerialis* and sometimes as a burgher. In fact, if it is true that the most important steps towards urban autonomy were taken during the period when the archbishop and the town were on

---

ministerialis family actually resident in Cologne appears to have been the von Bacheim family, the hereditary chamberlains (Lau, *Beamten*, p.47). Some facts in Pötter, *Die Ministerialität der Erzbischöfe von Köln* are useful, but he misses much also.

240. An edition of the *Dienstrecht* is given by Wilhelm Altmann and Ernst Bernheim, eds., *Ausgewählte Urkunden zur Erläuterung der Verfassungsgeschichte Deutschlands im Mittelalter*, 4th ed. (Berlin, 1909), no.83.

241. The way in which the transition from *ministerialis* to burgher probably took place is indicated by Hibbert and by Ganshof, p.59. The lower *ministeriales*, administering *ministeria* bound up with the new commerce and resident in the town, began to adopt the life style of the new mercantile group, invested in trade or local industry, bought urban property, and perhaps became merchants themselves. The corporate organization of the higher *ministeriales* and its regulation in the *Dienstrecht* gave the higher *ministeriales* a new sense of solidarity, but it also excluded the lower *ministeriales*. This made it all the more likely that the latter group would throw its lot in with the burghers.

relatively good terms, then the presence of some of his officials among the town leaders may have comforted him somewhat.

The *ministeriales* may not have been as numerous and influential in Cologne as Schulz has found them to have been in Worms and Trier,[242] but that is undoubtedly because Cologne was a more important center of long-distance trade than the other two cities. Still, Schulz's conclusions can be adopted for Cologne: *ministeriales* were active in urban life throughout the twelfth century and beyond; they were not alien elements, but burghers who shared in the common life and the common duties of the town. The proportion of *ministeriales* to others may have been smaller in Cologne than elsewhere, but the basic pattern seems to have been the same.

The *ministerialis* who became a merchant and a burgher is one possible explanation for the men who appear in the records as both *ministeriales* and burghers. Equally possible is a pattern where a merchant, of whatever origin, became a *ministerialis*. The ranks of the *ministeriales* were not suddenly flooded with new men in this period, as has sometimes been assumed;[243] but when new men were made *ministeriales*, it was more likely to happen among the urban *ministeriales*.

Certain individuals were clearly *ministeriales* who became burghers (see the accompanying table).[244] Richolf of Aachen is the most clear-cut case as well as the only imperial *ministerialis*. His uncle Karl the *thelonearius* and Karl's son of the same name are mentioned only once as *ministeriales*, but their family connection to Richolf and Karl's office make it likely that they, too, were of *ministerialis* origin. Another man, who has not been mentioned until now because he did not hold an office, but who fits the same pattern, was Hermann von Wighus (*a domo bellica*). He is mentioned frequently as a *ministerialis* of the abbey of St.

---

242. Schulz, "Die Ministerialität als Problem," pp.184–219, and *Ministerialität und Bürgertum in Trier* (Bonn, 1968).

243. Ahrens, pp.82ff., argues that there was not a massive influx of free men into the ranks of the *ministeriales* after 1150, but this need not affect conclusions on the urban *ministeriales* where one would expect to find more exceptions.

244. In what follows I am purposely excluding the *ministeriales* called Grin because they represent an entirely different line from the bourgeois Grin, a line whose genealogical connection with the bourgeois Grin cannot be established.

Pantaleon between 1141 and 1166, but in 1149 he was one of the bourgeois witnesses (*meliores*) to the craft gild regulation.[245]

The Raitze family, which remained prominent in the patriciate from the twelfth through the fourteenth century, also derived from a family of *ministeriales*. Razo of Suphtele is mentioned repeatedly as a *ministerialis* of St. Pantaleon. His son Hermann is listed as a *ministerialis* of the same abbey, and his grandson Heinrich appears as a *ministerialis* of the cathedral. If this prominence of *ministeriales* in the family is considered in conjunction with the virtual lack of circumstantial evidence for commercial activity, we may be fairly certain that the Raitze family was ministerial in origin.

The *thelonearii* constitute a special group of *ministeriales*. In addition to the Karl mentioned above, they were Werner, the "founder" of the Jude family, and Gerhard Ungemaz. The office of *thelonearius* had originally been a ministerial office, but it gradually lost that character. Thus the *thelonearii*, at first indistinguishable from other *ministeriales* in the charters, begin to appear at the head of the burghers in witness lists of the twelfth century, before the *scabini* but after the *ministeriales*. In this period (roughly 1150–1200) an occasional reference to them as *ministeriales* or the inclusion of them as witnesses of the rank of *ministeriales* may reflect their gradually changing circumstances. By 1200, the transition was complete and the *thelonearii* became indistinguishable from other burghers. But these three men were probably *ministeriales* in the full sense of the word. Both Werner (Jude) and his son Daniel were *thelonearii* before 1152 when the administration of the toll was reorganized. The toll had become hereditary, and the early Jude family members held the toll as a ministerial fief. The Jude family appears to have been a family of *ministeriales* who took advantage of their critical position in the town to enter commerce (remembering the vineyard in Remagen). The same cannot be said for Gerhard Ungemaz and Karl, both of whom administered the toll after 1152; but it should be remembered that Karl was related to Richolf of Aachen, and that Gerhard Ungemaz held land in Lawrence parish among the *ministeriales* and no market land in Martin parish.

In each of these cases the pattern seems clear enough. The Raitze and the Jude families as well as individuals like Richolf of Aachen, his uncle Karl, and Hermann von Wighus were burghers of certain or probable ministerial origin. Three other families pose a more difficult problem:

---

245. Lacomblet I 344 (1141), 352 (1144), 373 (1152), 378 (1153), 395 (1158), 425 (1166); von Loesch I 10 (1149).

the Minnevuz, Parfuse, and von Mummersloch. The Minnevuz and the Parfuse were both descended from Rainer of Basel and Bertradis von der Mühlengassen. Rainer's name and the fact the children inherited land primarily from their mother supports a mercantile, nonministerial origin. Yet three of Rainer's descendants, Gozwin Minnevuz and Richolf and Constantine Parfuse were *ministeriales* by the early thirteenth century. Perhaps this is an example of a merchant who was not a *ministerialis*, but whose descendants became *ministeriales* after a generation or two. The von Mummersloch family may fit the same pattern. Hermann von Mummersloch was the *Schultheiss* at Flittard in the 1180's for the abbot of St. Martin, but no other member of the family can be shown to have been a *ministerialis*.[246]

There can be no doubt that *ministeriales* played an important role in Cologne in the twelfth century; however, these men were not far different from the other prominent burghers. They were not officials imposed from outside, but men assimilated to one degree or another into the common life of the city. They formed an important part of the patriciate as did merchants of more humble origin.

---

246. Two further examples of dependency on an ecclesiastical foundation appear for political figures in the twelfth century. Hermann and Richwin Canus, who pertained to the *familia* of St. Martin, and Gottfried von Staveren, who probably pertained to the same *familia*. Usually *familia* is equivalent to all dependents, including the *ministeriales*, but in at least one twelfth-century source for St. Pantaleon (*Quellen* I 344: 1141) the *homines* and *ministeriales* of the abbey are listed separately from the *familia*. The Canus and Gottfried seem more likely to have been *ministeriales* but more specific information is lacking.

Chapter 6

Conclusions

The urban community in Cologne assumed a definite shape in the twelfth century. Although the documentary record is fragmentary, especially for the first half of the century, some conclusions can be drawn concerning the development of urban institutions and of political groups in the century.

The most important conclusion, which must be kept in mind if we are to evaluate the rest of the evidence properly, is that the urban community developed in a period which was for the most part free of local conflict. The general tranquillity of the twelfth century in Cologne is frequently obscured by the violent outbursts in 1074 and 1106 at the century's beginning and the great struggles with the archbishop in 1225 and the 1250's at its end. But, with a minor exception in 1138, there were no uprisings or bloody incidents in the period 1112–1225, and this is the period that was crucial for the development of the urban community.

To assess the rise of the community correctly we must focus on this long period of peace when the burghers were building the institutions that stood them in good stead in the thirteenth century. Revolt was one method used by the burghers, but it was not the only one and not, I believe, the most important one. It may be that in principle, or in terms of their "necessary" historical roles, the archbishop and the burghers were irreconcilably opposed to one another. Certainly they came into conflict even if it was not always bloody. But it is dangerous to reason from the level of a "necessary" historical role to the level of individual motivation or action. In fact, the archbishop and the community could and did cooperate.

The archbishops clearly did not concern themselves too much with the communal development in Cologne in the twelfth century; it might even be called a period of "salutary neglect." The best indication of this is the fortifications dispute of 1180.[1] Archbishop Philip demanded a payment because the fortifications had been built without his consent; in this way he reasserted his position as lord of the town. But he allowed the new fortifications to stand, even though they were undertaken to the detriment of his authority. The reason for such salutary neglect in the twelfth century lies in the political interests of the twelfth-century archbishops. Deeply involved in imperial affairs, by virtue of both their position and their personal connections, the archbishops of Cologne could not personally oversee the development of the urban community.

Furthermore, the archbishop did not really have an administration in Cologne that could govern in his absence. The events of 1074 show how weak his power was in the city. In that controversy the *Burggraf* was absent and the *Stadtvogt* was ineffective; the archbishop had to rely on support from the countryside. The institutions that developed in the twelfth century were built not on the basis of the archbishop's position as lord, but on the new community of Cologne. Although the lack of sources makes it impossible to know precisely how it came about, there seems little doubt that most of the important institutional developments of the twelfth century took place with the archbishop's approval, whether expressed or tacit.

But the institutional development of the twelfth century had two aspects. In the first place older institutions were modified to reflect the increased importance of the community. The *Burggraf* and the *Stadtvogt* were replaced on almost all occasions by the viscount and the subadvocate, who appear by 1106 and who were invariably bourgeois. By mid-century the *scabini* of the archbishop's high court took on additional duties as leaders of the urban community, meeting in the city hall with other prominent burghers or making decisions in a communal peace court. They kept the city seal, which also appears for the first time about 1150. The *scabini* were all bourgeois as well. Other men, who were dependent on the archbishop, through either their institutional position or personal loyalty or both, were also prominent in urban affairs in the twelfth century. Numerous *ministeriales* were active in urban life in the twelfth century, and archiepiscopal officials like the *thelonearii* were especially important. These men, too, were bourgeois. By the twelfth century no distinction can be made between the urban *ministeriales* and the burghers. The one urban community encompasses both groups.

---

1. *Quellen* I 94.

It is only speculation, but it may well be that the archbishops of the twelfth century could rest content with this aspect of institutional development. In a town that was growing rapidly the old lordship institutions, which had never been very effective, were clearly inadequate. Through the increasing power of his judicial officials and the important role of his *ministeriales*, the archbishop may have felt that his authority and power were being maintained at the same time that the changed institutions were better able to cope with the new problems. It must be emphasized again that there is no concrete evidence on the motivation of the individual archbishops in urban affairs in this period. There are no archiepiscopal documents establishing new institutional arrangements. But, even if the archbishops did not encourage the development, they did from all appearances condone it.[2]

But there was a second aspect to institutional change in Cologne in the twelfth century, and this aspect was ultimately the more dangerous one. This was the development of private associations with public functions. The parish communities were an established part of Cologne life in the early twelfth century, but gradually in the course of the century the parishioners' activities were restricted and replaced by the power of the parish magistrates and their gild. In the mid-twelfth century the *scabini* acted in conjunction with other prominent men as a communal authority. By 1180 a private organization, the *Richerzeche*, which was composed of some *scabini* and some other prominent men, had arisen. The *Richerzeche* performed some of the functions, especially gild regulation, which the *scabini* had previously performed. Even the *scabini* themselves developed a corporate organization in the twelfth century. These groups were less susceptible to control by the archbishop. Although there was little objection to them in the twelfth century, by the thirteenth century the archbishop saw them as a definite threat and demanded that they be restricted or disbanded. It is significant that the judges in the Great Arbitration of 1258, when speaking to this point, insisted that the *Richerzeche* was a legitimate institution and that it had the right to elect the *Bürgermeister* because it

---

2. Ecclesiastical leaders did sometimes encourage changes of direct value to the bourgeoisie. For example, Bishop Bertram of Metz (1180–97) instituted parish officials in each parish to guarantee contracts. Bertram had come to Metz from Cologne and modeled his reforms on the Cologne system (cf. Schneider, p.101). In general many of the observations made by Schneider for Metz hold true for Cologne, even though the cities differed greatly. In Cologne, however, there is no documentary evidence that the archbishop actually instituted any of the major changes.

was established by time-honored custom. Generally the judges in 1258 were sympathetic to the archbishop, but not at this point. The period of salutary neglect in the twelfth century had left an important legacy.[3]

An urban community and communal institutions developed in the twelfth century, but it is doubtful that a formal commune existed. There is no evidence of a communal oath or of a town council of *iurati* in this period. Those who insist that a revolutionary commune existed from 1106 on are forced to regard it as a clandestine organization in the twelfth century which only gained a fully public position in the thirteenth century. Such a view is based on analogy to the communal development in other cities, but it strains the evidence from Cologne too much. Furthermore, it is founded on the assumption that the archbishop and the urban community were irreconcilable enemies. Yet even where a formal commune did exist in northern Europe in the late eleventh and twelfth centuries, it was an association of peace, not a revolutionary organization, as Vermeesch has shown for the early urban communes of

---

3. Lacomblet II 452, arts. 1,2: Proponit archiepiscopus Colon. predictus, quod in ciuitate Colon., in qua est summus iudex tam spiritualium quam temporalium tota jurisdictio tam spiritualium quam temporalium dependet ab ipso. Quod in ipsa ciuitate Colon. nemo potest iuste sibi iurisdictionem aliquam vendicare, nisi eam habeat ab ipso archiepiscopo.

Art. 42: Quod officiales de Richerzecheit in domo ciuium conuenientes, inscio ipso archiepiscopo, statuunt quicquid volunt, et statutum tale volunt pro speciali consuetudine et iure seruari, ipsius archiepiscopi minime adhibita auctoritate.

The judges responded to articles 1 and 2 and, by implication, to article 42, in part, as follows: They agree that all authority in the town derives from the archbishop, but they go on to say, ". . . sunt tamen . . . sub ipso et ab ipso iudices iurisdictionem habentes, et officiati, qui dicuntur magistri ciuium, qui ex consuetudine ab antiquo seruata eliguntur a fraternitate, que Richerzecheit vocatur, qui iurant facere et obseruare quasdam ordinationes, que in littera super hoc conscripta continentur. Quas si faciunt et obseruant secundum formam iuramenti, quod prestant quando ponuntur, dicimus hoc multum valere ad conseruationem ciuitatis. . . ." Still there had been numerous complaints against the *Richerzeche* and the *Bürgermeister*; therefore, the judges insist on an oath: ". . . ordinamus et diffinimus, quod de cetero illi, qui eligunt magistros ciuium, corporale iuramentum prestent, quod nec prece, nec pretio, nec affectu sanguinis vel affinitatis eligant, sed solo intuitu iustitie tales, qui secundum suam conscientiam utiliores sint rei publice. . . ."

northern France.[4] If the bishop of Amiens could support a commune for reasons of peace, it is not beyond the realm of possibility that the archbishops of Cologne could have sponsored the less radical measures taken there.

A revolutionary commune was not the basis for the urban community in Cologne in the twelfth century. Instead the basis for the community lay in the urban court.[5] The *scabini*, not a board of *iurati*, appear as town leaders in the twelfth century. Ownership of land within the confines of the town, not an oath, made one a member of the community and bound one to the principle of mutual protection. The predominant role of the community presented by the town records is the assurance that the citizens of Cologne would remain secure in the possession of their property and that whatever conflicts might arise would be adjudicated peacefully. This aspect of urban development, together with such evidence as the city seal, suggests a connection to the peace movement.[6]

But, if the urban court was the basis for the community, it should not seem surprising that the members of the community, and its leaders,

---

4. Vermeesch makes this point repeatedly, notably in the cases of Le Mans (p.88), St. Quentin (p.102), Noyon (p.107), Laon (p.112), and Amiens (p.114). He also shows the danger of relying too heavily on the condemnation of communes by one conservative cleric, Guibert of Nogent (p.109).

5. This is the thesis of Franz Steinbach. Cf. Steinbach, "Zur Sozialgeschichte," p.179: Nicht der Schwurverband sondern die Gerichtsgemeinde wurde noch um die Mitte des 12. Jahrhunderts regelmässig dreimal im Jahr als Bürgerschaftsversammlung zusammengerufen, um unter Vorsitz der Burggrafen im ganzen Stadtbereich ausserhalb und innerhalb der Mauern Recht zu weisen. Sie war M(eines) E(rachtens) die Urquelle der bürgerlichen Freiheitsrechte.

6. The seal, with its ecclesiastical symbols, was even used occasionally by the archbishop in the early thirteenth century in matters that seem to have little connection to the bourgeoisie. In 1203 Archbishop Adolf renewed an alliance with the Duke of Lorraine to which were affixed his own seal, that of the priors of Cologne, and the city seal (Lacomblet II 9). In 1222 Archbishop Engelbert received fiefs from the Duke of Brabant and had the transaction confirmed with his own seal and that of the citizens of Cologne (Lacomblet II 105). The archbishop would scarcely have allowed the city seal to be used if he had regarded it as the symbol of a revolutionary commune. It represented, instead, the communal "peace" of Cologne.

should represent a broad spectrum of social groups. Merchants, *ministeriales*, even clerics—anyone who held property in Cologne was a member of the urban community. Merchants must surely have played a major role in a town as involved in long-distance trade as Cologne was. But they were members of the urban community because they were landholders, not because they were merchants. The same is true of the *ministeriales*; some of them achieved an important position in the town because they held property there, not because they were dependents of the archbishop. If the basis of the urban community was the urban court and the possession of property within its jurisdiction, it is natural to look for a group of old, free landholders as the basis for urban rights. Possibly some of the burghers of the twelfth century were descendants of old freemen, but such a connection cannot be demonstrated. And there is no evidence that freemen who might have owned large tracts of land in the town before its dramatic expansion became the leaders of the town in the twelfth century. The court community was central, but those who comprised it in the twelfth century appear to have come from various places and from various social ranks. What these diverse individuals had in common was a bourgeois way of life and membership in the urban community.

Within the urban community certain men and certain families rose to prominence. From the beginning there had been "better men" in the town, but there was a tendency towards concentration of power in the later twelfth century. Major steps in this were the control gained by the parish gilds over the election of the parish masters and the new prominence of the *Bürgermeister* elected by the *Richerzeche*. The selection of most town officials passed into the hands of private corporations and the commonalty was pushed into the background. Since overlapping membership in these privileged bodies was common, all of the factors for a patriciate, in the sense of a political elite, were present by about 1200.

The origins of the patriciate were similar to the origins of the urban community as a whole. They came from diverse groups, as far as we can tell, and maintained their preeminent position in the town through their wealth, family connections, and political influence. There was a more restricted circle of patrician families in the thirteenth century than in the twelfth century, but the Cologne patriciate was never a completely closed group. The rise of the patriciate is closely associated with the development of communal institutions, especially those institutions where private gilds of officials arose. Many individuals and families enjoyed prominence before the private organizations were fully developed, but it was the private organizations that restricted the size of the group of prominent families and solidified the control the patriciate exercised. And the first crucial steps in this direction were taken in the twelfth century, in the period when the archbishops gave broad latitude to the independent development of urban institutions.

The archbishop complained in the Great Arbitration of 1258 that political office in Cologne was too often gained through family connections, payments to gild officials, and the like. Here the judges supported him; they, too, deplored the state of affairs where everyone seemed concerned about the game of patrician politics and no one was concerned for the health of the *res publica*. But such complaints were in vain. The patriciate had consolidated its position in the peace of the twelfth century, and its hold on the city was not even shaken, let alone broken, until the latter half of the fourteenth century.

Peaceful relations between the archbishop and the town came to an end after 1200 not only because urban institutions had developed in a specific way but also because the archbishop's position in the empire had changed. The influence of the empire in northwestern Germany declined dramatically from the 1190's on. The double election of 1198, the consciously weak policy of Frederick II in the area, and the interregnum after 1250 mark the progressive deterioration of imperial authority. In the process the archbishop became more a local prince than an imperial agent. As such, he was more keenly aware of the deficiencies in his control over the various groups in his lands, including the new town community. In the attempt to consolidate his power, he ran up against the rights and privileges established in the preceding century.

In retrospect, the reign of Philip of Heinsberg (1167–91) marks a turning point. Had the empire not collapsed in the half century after his death, perhaps his interest in consolidation would not appear so important; but it did collapse, and his successors continued along the lines of the policies he had established. Philip became an opponent of the emperor after he received the duchy of Westphalia and Engern. Much of his time and energy was devoted to bringing this region under his control. With the lands of Henry the Lion came a certain Welf disposition, which was strengthened by Cologne's commercial ties to England. But Philip was reconciled with the emperor in 1188 and remained loyal until his death in 1191. Furthermore, unlike later archbishops, Philip never came into any real conflict with the town.

The urban community was not the only group with vested interests the archbishops encountered when they attempted to consolidate their power in the thirteenth century. The development of the urban community must be seen as one of several "communities" which defined themselves. The basis for a sense of territoriality in the lands of the archbishop and for the later status groups of the territorial state was laid in the twelfth century.

In the eleventh and early twelfth centuries, in the charters of the archbishop of Cologne, lay witnesses were usually divided into two categories: freemen and *ministeriales*. The designations varied. In 1061 the distinction is drawn between knights (*milites*) and servants (*servientes*); in 1106 between nobles (*nobiles*) and the *familia* of St. Peter; and in 1116 between freemen (*liberi*) and *ministeriales*.[7] In essence these designations expressed the same thing, a distinction between men who were free and those who were not. As the archbishop was able to extend and tighten his territorial control, especially through feudal institutions, the first group came to include more and more counts who had important holdings in and near his duchies. These men are called nobles more often in the twelfth century than before. By the end of the century the formulas of the archiepiscopal documents make it clear that these nobles are regarded as the leaders of a territorial entity corresponding to the duchies held by the archbishop and that this territory has boundaries. This kind of formula becomes prevalent under Philip of Heinsberg but is already present under earlier archbishops, such as Arnold II and Rainald of Dassel. In 1188 Philip settled a dispute with the count of Cleves over an island in the lower Rhine between Wissel and Rees. Philip claimed that the land in question was his by synodal right since it was within the boundaries of his diocese and his by secular right since it was within the boundaries of his duchy.[8] In 1197 Adolf reported that Philip had purchased a number of important properties from the *Landgraf* Ludwig earlier "for the protection of the land (*terra*) and for the sake of peace."[9]

The concept is clear in the twelfth-century documents: there is a territory or land under the archbishop's control which has definite boundaries and whose most important leaders are the "nobles" (or in the thirteenth century the "magnates") of the land. The phrase *nobiles*

7. Lacomblet I 197, 267, 280.

8. Lacomblet I 511: . . . quia intra nostri episcopatus terminos iure synodali et nostre potestatis ducatus iure forensi consederat nostre ditione addicari et per quendam nostrum fidelem ministerialem circumsigniri precepimus. . . .

9. Lacomblet I 554: Philippus ob munitionem terre et pacem ecclesiarum pactus est pro tribus milibus marcarum et quingentis marcis. . . .

terrae appears for the first time in 1166.[10] From the time of Archbishop Adolf, it becomes increasingly common. But, even before the unmistakable phrase *nobiles terrae* is used, certain phrases suggest that the nobles were assuming a dominant position; In 1138 Arnold II referred to the nobles and "captains." In 1140 a decision was reached after counsel with the priors, the princes, the vassals, and the *ministeriales*.[11] Referring to the nobles as "captains" or "princes" did not become common, but the phrases do seem to foreshadow the later use of "nobles of the land."

Certainly it was the intention of the archbishops to construct from the counts and other important men in their duchies a status group who should serve the land's interests at a higher level than that of the *ministeriales*, who had constituted a separate status group for some time. The archbishops were not able to force their counts to submit, even if they were their vassals, as fully as they would have liked. But by the end of the twelfth century, conceptions of status and rank clearly predominate in the documents.

The priors of Cologne, along with the priors of Bonn, Xanten, and, later, Soest, had the same status in ecclesiastical society as the nobles of the land in lay society. The term makes its first appearance in the records about 1090. By the end of the twelfth century the archbishop alone had the right to fill a vacancy among the priors. But, during the course of the century, they had formed a college and had acquired the right to accept or reject any nominee presented to them, however he was chosen. The priors, along with the dean and *seniores* of the cathedral chapter and the nobles of the land, normally elected the archbishop.[12]

The nobles of the land and the priors assumed an identity and some form of organization, however loose, in the twelfth century, at the same time the *ministeriales* and the burghers were establishing new arrangements. The *ministeriales* had their rights confirmed in the *Dienstrecht*; already the greater *ministeriales* had acquired the lands and titles that

---

10. Lacomblet I 414.

11. Lacomblet I 328: ... presentibus personis canonicis attestantibus nobilibus capitaneis et de familia b. petri legalibus et bonis testimonii iuris. . . .

Lacomblet I 341: ... consilio priorum suorum principum hominum et ministerialium. . . .

12. Oediger, p.246.

eventually distinguished them from the rest of the *ministeriales* and turned them into knights. The burghers had organized to exercise and protect their rights and had introduced new procedures and methods. Viewed from this perspective, the urban community no longer appears so unusual.

Too often medieval towns are viewed as phenomena which were in, but not of, the Middle Ages. Supposedly they represented new values and new concepts of human organization which set them off completely from contemporary landed society. If this perspective is discarded, the actual development of a town like Cologne can be seen more accurately. There is a certain transitional character, a kind of duality, to the twelfth century in Cologne. The archbishop's lordship existed side by side with communal institutions condoned by the archbishop. *Ministeriales* rubbed shoulders with free burghers, and, in fact, the two groups were almost indistinguishable in the town. The old lordship system was not dead, and the new communal system was not fully established as an autonomous system of organization. But it was precisely this period of peaceful transition, this period of duality, that laid the foundation for the bourgeois community of Cologne in the Middle Ages.

Bibliography

Sources and Source Collections

Altmann, Wilhelm and Ernst Bernheim, eds. *Ausgewählte Urkunden zur Erläuterung der Verfassungsgeschichte Deutschlands im Mittelalter.* 4th ed. Berlin: Weidmann, 1909.

"Annales Colonienses Brevissimi," *MGH. SS.* I. Edited by Georg Heinrich Pertz. Hannover: Hahn, 1826. P.79.

"Annales Colonienses Maximi," *MGH. SS.* XVII. Edited by Karl Pertz. Hannover: Hahn, 1861. Pp.729–847.

"Annales Egmundani," *MGH. SS.* XVI. Edited by Georg Heinrich Pertz. Hannover: Hahn, 1859. Pp.443–479.

"Annales Fuldenses," *MGH. SS.* I. Edited by Georg Heinrich Pertz. Hannover: Hahn, 1826. Pp.343–415.

"Annales Hildesheimenses," *MGH. SS.* III. Edited by Georg Heinrich Pertz. Hannover: Hahn, 1839. Pp.22, 42–70, 90–116.

Beyer, Heinrich, Leopold Eltester, and Adam Goerz, eds. *Urkundenbuch zur Geschichte der jetzt die Preussischen Regierungsbezirke Coblenz und Trier bildenden mittelrheinischen Territorien.* 2 vols. Coblenz: Hölscher, 1865.

Buyken, Thea, and Hermann Conrad, eds. *Die Amtleutebücher der kölnischen Sondergemeinden.* Weimar: Böhlau, 1936. (Publikationen der Gesellschaft für rheinische Geschichtskunde, 45.)

Caesarius of Heisterbach. *Dialogus Miraculorum.* Edited by Josef Strange. Köln-Bonn-Brussels: Heberle, 1851.

"Continuator Reginonis," *MGH. SS.* I. Edited by Georg Heinrich Pertz. Hannover: Hahn, 1826. Pp.614–629.

Ennen, Leonhard and Gottfried Eckertz, eds. *Quellen zur Geschichte der Stadt Köln.* 6 vols. Köln: DuMont- Schauberg, 1863–79.

Guiraud, Jean, ed. *Les Régistres d'Urbain IV.* 3 vols. Paris: Fontemoing, 1899–1904.

Höhlbaum, Konstantin, ed. *Hansisches Urkundenbuch.* 4 vols. Halle: Waidmann, 1876–96.

Hoeniger, Robert, ed. *Kölner Schreinskarten des zwölften Jahrhunderts.* 2 vols. Bonn: Weber, 1884–94.

Joerres, P., ed. *Urkundenbuch des Stiftes St. Gereon zu Köln.* Bonn: Hanstein, 1893.

Knipping, Richard, ed. *Die Regesten der Erzbishchöfe von Köln im Mittelalter.* 2 vols. Bonn: Hanstein, 1901–13.

———. "Ungedruckte Urkunden der Erzbischöfe von Köln aus dem 12. und 13. Jahrhundert," *Annalen* 74 (1902), pp.179–194; 75 (1903), pp.112–142.

Korth, Leonard, ed. *Liber privilegiorum maioris ecclesie Coloniensis: Der älteste Kartular des Kölner Domstiftes.* Trier: Lintz, 1886. (*Westdeutsche Zeitschrift für Geschichte und Kunst, Ergänzungsheft 3.*)

———. "Urkunden aus dem Stadtarchiv von Köln," *Annalen* 41 (1884), pp.72–182.

Lacomblet, Theodor, ed. *Urkundenbuch für die Geschichte des Niederrheins.* 4 vols. Düsseldorf: Elberfeld, 1840–58.

Lambert of Hersfeld. "Annales," *MGH. SS.* V. Edited by L. F. Hessius. Hannover: Hahn, 1843. Pp.134–263.

Lantbert. "Vita Heriberti," *MGH. SS.* IV. Edited by Georg Heinrich Pertz. Hannover: Hahn, 1841. Pp.740–753.

Piot, Charles, ed. *Cartulaire de l'abbaye de saint-Trond.* 2 vols. Brussels: Hayez, 1870–74.

Planitz, Hans, and Thea Buyken, eds. *Die Kölner Schreinsbücher des 13. und 14. Jahrhunderts.* Weimar: Böhlau, 1937. (Publikationen der Gesellschaft für rheinische Geschichtskunde, 46.)

Ruotger. "Vita Brunonis," *MGH. SS.* IV. Edited by Georg Heinrich Pertz. Hannover: Hahn, 1841. Pp.254–275.

Schäfer, Heinrich, ed. "Inventare und Regesten aus den Kölner Pfarrarchiven, *Annalen* 71 (1901), 83 (1907).

Sickel, Theodor, ed. *MGH. DD.* I, II. Hannover: Hahn, 1879–93.

Von Loesch, Heinrich, ed. *Die Kölner Zunfturkunden nebst anderen Kölner Gewerbeurkunden bis zum Jahre 1500.* 2 vols. Bonn: Hanstein,

1907. (Publikationen der Gesellschaft für rheinische Geschichtskunde, 22.)

Weiland, Ludwig, ed. *MGH. LL.* Section 4 (*Constitutiones*) vols. 1,2. Hannover: Hahn, 1893–96.

Secondary Works

Ahrens, Jacob. *Die Ministerialität in Köln und am Niederrhein.* Leipzig: Quelle und Meyer, 1908. (Leipziger Historische Abhandlungen, 9.)

Beyerle, Konrad. "Die Anfänge des Kölner Schreinswesens," *ZRG* 51 (1931), pp.318–509.

———. "Die Entstehung der Stadtgemeinde Köln," *ZRG* 31 (1910), pp.1–67.

———. *Die Urkundenfälschungen des Kölner Burggrafen Heinrich III. von Arberg.* Heidelberg: Winter, 1913. (Deutschrechtliche Beiträge, 9, heft 4.)

Dollinger, Philippe. "Patriciat noble et patriciat bourgeois à Strasbourg au XIVe siècle," *Revue d'Alsace* 90 (1950–51), pp.52–82.

———. "Les Villes allemandes au moyen âge: les groupements sociaux," *La Ville* II. Brussels: Editions de la libraire encyclopédique, 1955. Pp.371–401. (Recueils de la Société Jean Bodin, 7.)

Eheberg, Karl Theodor. *Ueber das ältere deutsche Münzwesen und die Hausgenossenschaften besonders in volkswirtschaftlicher Beziehung.* Leipzig: Dunkler und Humbolt, 1879.

Ennen, Edith. "The Different Types of Formation of European Towns," *Early Medieval Society.* Translated and edited by Sylvia Thrupp. New York: Appleton-Century-Crofts, 1967. Pp.174–182. (Originally: "Les Différents Types de formation des villes européennes," *Le Moyen Age* 62 (1956), pp.397–411.)

———. *Frühgeschichte der europäischen Stadt.* Bonn: Röhrscheidt, 1953.

Febvre, Lucien, Jean Lestocquoy, and Georges Espinas. "Fils de Riches ou Nouveaux Riches," *AESC* 1 (1946), pp.139–153.

Föhl, Walther. "Studien zu Rainald von Dassel," *Jahrbücher des kölnischen Geschichtsvereins* 17 (1935), pp.234–259, 20 (1938), pp.238–260.

Ganshof, François-Louis. *Etude sur les ministeriales en Flandre et en Lotharingie.* Brussels: Lamertin, 1926. (Académie royale de Belgique, classe des lettres et des sciences morales et politiques. Mémoires, 2nd sér., 20.)

Hampe, Karl. *Deutsche Kaisergeschichte in der Zeit der Salier und Staufer.* 11th ed., revised by Friedrich Baethgen. Heidelberg: Quelle und Meyer, 1963.

Hansay, Alfred. "L'origine du patriciat à Liège au moyen âge," *RBPH* 2 (1923), pp.696–701.

Hegel, Eduard. "Die Entstehung des mittelalterlichen Pfarrsystems der Stadt Köln," *Kölner Untersuchungen: Festgabe zur 1900-Jahrfeier der Stadtgründung.* Edited by Walther Zimmermann. Rathingen: Henn, 1950. Pp.69–89. (*Die Kunstdenkmäler im Landesteil Nordrhein*, Beihang 2.)

Hegel, Karl. *Die Entstehung des deutschen Städtewesens.* Leipzig: Hirzel, 1898.

Hibbert, Arthur B. "The Origin of the Medieval Town Patriciate," *Past and Present*, no.3 (Feb. 1953), pp.15–27.

Hoeniger, Robert. "Die älteste Urkunde der Kölner Richerzeche," *Mevissenfestschrift.* Köln: DuMont-Schauberg, 1895. Pp.253–298.

Keussen, Hermann. *Topographie der Stadt Köln im Mittelalter.* 2 vols. und Karten. Bonn: Hanstein, 1910.

Koebner, Richard. *Die Anfänge des Gemeinwesens der Stadt Köln.* Bonn: Hanstein, 1922.

Latouche, Robert. *The Birth of the Western Economy.* Translated by E. M. Wilkinson. London: Methuen, 1961. (Originally: *Les Origines de l'économie occidentale.* Paris: Editions Albin Michel, 1956.)

Lau, Friedrich. *Entwicklung der kommunalen Verfassung und Verwaltung der Stadt Köln bis zum Jahre 1396.* Bonn: Behrendt, 1898.

——. *Die erzbischöflichen Beamten in der Stadt Köln während des zwölften Jahrhunderts.* Lübeck: Schmidt, 1891.

——. "Das Kölner Patriziat bis zum Jahre 1325," *Mitteilungen* 24 (1893), pp.71–89; 25 (1894), pp.358–381; 26 (1895), pp.103–157.

——. "Das Schöffenkollegium des Hochgerichts zu Köln bis zum Jahre 1396," *Mevissenfestschrift.* Köln: DuMont-Schauberg, 1895. Pp.107–130.

Lestocquoy, Jean. *Les Villes de Flandre et d'Italie sous le gouvernement des patriciens (XIe–XIVe siècles).* Paris: Presses Universitaires, 1952.

Maschke, Erich. "Continuité sociale et histoire urbaine médiévale," *AESC* 15 (1960), pp.936–948.

Mundy, John. *Liberty and Political Power in Toulouse, 1050–1230.* New York: Columbia University Press, 1954.

Oediger, Frederich-Wilhelm and Wilhelm Neuss. *Geschichte des Erzbistums*

Köln, I: Das Bistum Köln von den Anfängen bis zum Ende des 12. Jahrhunderts. Köln: Bachem, 1964.

Perrin, Charles-Edmond. "L'évolution d'une monnaie: le denier de Cologne," *AHES* 4 (1932), pp.194–197.

Philippi, Friedrich, "Die Kölner Richerzeche," *Mitteilungen des Instituts für österreichische Geschichtsforschung* 32 (1911), pp.87–112.

Pirenne, Henri. "Commune, Medieval," *Encyclopedia of the Social Sciences* 4. New York: Macmillan, 1931. Pp.61–63.

———. "The Stages in the Social History of Capitalism," *AHR* 19 (1913–14), pp.494–515.

Planitz, Hans. *Die deutsche Stadt im Mittelalter.* Köln-Graz: Böhlau, 1954.

———. "Die deutsche Stadtgemeinde," *ZRG* 64 (1944), pp.1–85.

———. "Die Frühgeschichte der deutschen Stadt," *ZRG* 63 (1943), pp.1–91.

———. "Kaufmannsgilde und städtische Eidgenossenschaft in niederfränkischen Städten im 11. und 12. Jahrhundert," *ZRG* 60 (1940), pp.1–116.

———. "Konstitutivakt und Eintragung in der Kölner Schreinsurkunden des 12. und 13. Jahrhunderts," *Festschrift für Alfred Schultze.* Edited by Walther Merk. Weimar: Böhlau, 1934. Pp.175–205.

Pötter, Wilhelm. *Die Ministerialität der Erzbischöfe von Köln vom Ende des 11. bis zum Ausgang des 13. Jahrhunderts.* Düsseldorf: Schwann, 1967. (Studien zur Kölner Kirchengeschichte, 9.)

Rothert, Hermann. *Westfälische Geschichte, I: Das Mittelalter.* 2nd ed. Gütersloh: Bertelsmann, 1962.

Rütimeyer, Elisabeth. *Stadtherr und Stadtbürgerschaft in den rheinischen Bischofsstädten: Ihr Kampf um die Hoheitsrechte im Hochmittelalter.* Stuttgart: Kohlhammer, 1928. (*VSWG*, Beiheft 13.)

Saabe, Etienne. "Quelques Types de marchandes des IXe et Xe siècles," *RBPH* 13 (1934), pp.176–187.

Schmoller, Gustav. *Deutsches Städtewesen in älterer Zeit.* Bonn-Leipzig: Schroeder, 1922. (Bonner Staatswissenschaftliche Untersuchungen, 5.)

Schneider, Jean. *La Ville de Metz aux XIIIe et XIVe siècles.* Nancy: Thomas, 1950.

Schulz, Knut. "Die Ministerialität als Problem der Stadtgeschichte: Einige allgemeine Bermerkungen, erläutert am Beispiel der Stadt Worms," *Rheinische Vierteljahrsblätter* 32 (1968), pp.184–219.

———. *Ministerialität und Bürgertum in Trier: Untersuchungen zur recht-*

lichen und sozialen Gliederung der Trierer Bürgerschaft. Bonn: Rheinisches Archiv, 1968.

Seeliger, Gerhard. *Studien zur älteren Verfassungsgeschichte Köln: Zwei Urkunden des Kölner Erzbischofs von 1169.* Leipzig: Teubner, 1909. (Abhandlungen der sächsischen Gesellschaft der Wissenschaften, phil.-hist. Klasse, 26.)

Steinbach, Franz. "Stadtgemeinde und Landgemeinde: Studien zur Geschichte des Bürgertums I," *Rheinische Vierteljahrsblätter*, Jahrgang 13 (1948), pp.11—50.

———. *Der Ursprung der Kölner Stadtgemeinde.* Bonn: Hanstein, 1955. (Vorträge der Gesellschaft für rheinische Geschichtskunde, 10.)

———. "Zur Sozialgeschichte von Köln im Mittelalter," *Spiegel der Geschichte: Festgabe für Max Braubach zum 10. April 1964.* Edited by Konrad Repgen and Stephan Skalwert. Münster: Aschendorff, 1964. Pp.171—197.

Van Werveke, Hans. *Gand: Esquisse d'histoire sociale.* Brussels: Renaissance du Livre, 1946.

Vermeesch, Albert. *Essai sur les origines et la signification de la commune dans le nord de la France (XIe et XIIIe siècles).* Heule: UGA, 1966. (Etudes Présentées à la Commission Internationale pour l'Histoire des Assemblées d'Etats, 30.)

Von Klocke, Friedrich. *Das Patriziatsproblem und die Werler Erbsälzer.* Münster: Aschendorff, 1965.

Von Loesch, Heinrich. "Die Grundlagen der ältesten Kölner Gemeindeverfassung," *ZRG* 53 (1933), pp.89—207.

———. *Die Kölner Kaufmannsgilde im zwölften Jahrhundert.* Trier: Lintz, 1904. (*Westdeutsche Zeitschrift für Geschichte und Kunst,* Ergänzungsheft 12.)

Von Winterfeld, Luise. "Gottesfrieden und deutsche Stadtverfassung," *Hansische Geschichtsblätter*, Jahrgang 1927, pp.8—56.

———. *Handel, Kapital, und Patriziat in Köln bis 1400.* Lübeck: Schmidt-Römhild, 1925. (Pfingstblätter des hansischen Geschichtsvereins, 16.)

———. "Neue Untersuchungen über die Anfänge des Gemeinwesens der Stadt Köln," *VSWG* 18 (1924—25), pp.1—25.

Witt, Ronald G. "The Landlord and the Economic Revival of the Middle Ages in Northern Europe, 1000—1250," *AHR* 76 (1971), pp. 965—988.

Index